WHEN HUSBANDS DIE

WHEN HUSBANDS DIE

Women Share Their Stories

Shirley Reeser McNally

with
Barbara Harrison Mulhern
and
Mary Witt Wydman

SUNSTONE PRESS

SANTA FE

Sunstone books may be purchased for educational, business, or sales promotional use. For information please write: Special Markets Department, Sunstone Press, P.O. Box 2321, Santa Fe, New Mexico 87504-2321.

Library of Congress Cataloging-in-Publication Data:

McNally, Shirley Reeser, 1925-
  When husbands die : women share their stories / Shirley Reeser McNally with Barbara Harrison Mulhern and Mary Witt Wydman.
    p. cm.
  ISBN 0-86534-442-6 (softcover)
1. Widows—United States—Psychology. 2. Widows—United States—Case studies. 3. Widowhood—United States. 4. Husbands—Death—Psychological aspects. 5. Loss (Psychology)
I. Mulhern, Barbara Harrison. II. Wydman, Mary Witt. III. Title.

HQ1058.5.U5M35 2005
155.6′4433—dc22
                              2004026789

Published in

WWW.SUNSTONEPRESS.COM
SUNSTONE PRESS / POST OFFICE BOX 2321 / SANTA FE, NM 87504-2321 /USA
(505) 988-4418 / *ORDERS ONLY* (800) 243-5644 / FAX (505) 988-1025

Contents

On the Cover: Walking in Ireland, Smith College Travel: Coming down from the Burren's "hilly grey expanse of jagged peaks and slippery steeps." (Quote from *The Book of the Burren*, published by Tir Eolas, Ireland.) Ahead are the green growing fields of that beautiful country. (Photo by Euphemia Steffey)

☙ Acknowledgments ❧

Our deepest thanks go to the women of Smith College, Northampton, Massachusetts, who have shared their stories for the purposes of this project, to the scholars who have assisted us, and to other friends who have offered their insight about what happens to women in today's society as they learn to survive and make new lives for themselves when their husbands die.

—Shirley Reeser McNally, Class of 1947
—Barbara Harrison Mulhern, Class of 1947
—Mary Witt Wydman, Class of 1947

⤜ Introduction ⤛

When Husbands Die has evolved as a sharing of personal reactions, recollections and relationships by women who are living through the enormous life change they faced when, in an instant, through no action, choice or fault of their own, they became widows. It is offered in the hope that other widows will find within its pages survivors like themselves who can help them on their life journeys to the good places that are attainable.

It is also for families, to help them understand what is happening to the mother, sister, daughter they think they know so well. It is also for friends, to let them know how strong or weak, needy, isolated or emotionally exhausted their good old pals really are and will continue to be for weeks, months, and years to come.

And it is for people who are still married, to ask them—to beg them—to learn, to understand, to leave denial for a time and face the reality of their own deaths and what they can do, now, to help the one who will be left behind.

The stories told by the women who responded to the project's questionnaire are poignant, sad, disturbing and, in many ways, healing. Every story is personal. Each person's grief is personal; it is grief that will not be relegated to a studied, step-by-step process. Unless you have experienced the grief unique to this situation, you cannot explain what it's like. Unless you have to live it, as several women said, you cannot understand it. There are some generalities, but grief work and recovery are open-ended.

We take our own steps. We stumble and then we go on, each in our own way. We can learn from others. The stories women are willing to share may well become vital to your own progress after the death of your husband—through your grief and mourning, through changing relationships with friends and family, through solutions of financial matters, to the necessary reinvention of yourself.

The women who shared in this project have become our friends, more than that, in the way of women, they have become our sisters. They may become yours. Their stories will bring solace and support for your own experiences and misgivings. If you do not see yourself in every response, that's because you are not there. Each situation has its own specifics; no two are any more alike than the storytellers themselves. There are similarities; there are common threads. You will find them. You also will find humor, strength, despair, encouragement, honesty and above all, hope. Use the stories to learn about yourself: about the person you are becoming, the work you must do. More than seventy-nine women are sharing their thoughts with you to help you move from one part of your life to another. They, too, have been suddenly singled—made single—and forced into an unwanted life change: to be wives no longer, to become widows when their husbands died. Each of them had to learn to live without her lover, her best friend, her partner, her companion—and her marriage!

—Shirley McNally, Santa Fe, New Mexico

1

⤜ The Project ⤛
Begin at the Beginning

Women whose husbands have died feel a kinship. They are proof, one for the other, that survival is possible. The women who share their stories here do so in hopes that they will be of help to women who are preparing for or experiencing the months and years of trauma that follow the tragic loss when husbands die. While the mutuality of this loss is not a particularly positive beginning for a friendship, it is an opportunity to share experiences and moments of empathy or sympathy, as well as moments of great strength that may be helpful and healing.

The basis for the friendship among the three of us who began this project, Barbara Harrison Mulhern, Mary Witt Wydman and Shirley Reeser McNally, is our four years at Smith College, a women's liberal arts institution in Massachusetts. Although we were in the same college class and knew each other, we were not close companions during those college years, nor did we maintain a relationship following graduation.

By June of 1989, when the story of this project begins, we had each outlived our husbands. Bob Wydman died in 1984, Art Mulhern died in 1986, Jerry McNally, my husband, died early in 1989. Old school friends and current strangers, Mary, Barbara and I were about to become deeply involved. Quite independently, each of us had developed concern for the many women who, like ourselves, will have to experience great loss and trauma when their husbands die and they must move to a solitary way of life after years of marriage. How we came together and what we want to share about our own experiences are part of the story.

⤳ ⤳ ⤳ ⤳

Shirley Reeser McNally, 1991

Jerry McNally died at home, around two o'clock on the morning of February 9, 1989. We had fought his cancer for three years. With his death, all of us—husband, wife, son, daughter and son-in-law—were freed from the cancer. The consequences of that death were many. One of them, a major one, was that I was no longer married. In an instant, I had become, in society's eyes and labeling, if not yet my own, a single person. This happened because of circumstances far beyond my control. It was an appalling reality!

Soon after Jerry's death, I began to write about my feelings: the frustrations, the problems, the misunderstandings, the despair and the changes. I made notes about the vulnerability I continued to experience, the anguish, the confusion, the deeply felt need to talk about him—and about the love and support I received from expected and unexpected sources.

I asked myself many questions. Were my reactions typical? Were the fatigue, the lack of focus, the sense of isolation, the moments of mindlessness, the intense loneliness, the sudden termination of my position as partner and caretaker, the horror of this unwanted move from married woman to widow as devastating to other women as they were to me? Did everyone experience the quick and overwhelming rush of tears? The anguish? Could I bear the awful loss of intimacy, the absence of his touching me, the impossibility of my being able to touch him in our own gentle, meaningful ways? Not to feel him next to me in bed, not to hear his breathing? The forever of it was impossible to accept.

How were our adult children dealing with their own grief? They had lost their father. What were their concerns about the new status of their mother? What did they expect of me? What could I expect of them? Our daughter and her husband were wonderfully available. Our son was silent and often absent.

Was what I was experiencing normal? Was there any norm? There was real physical pain. There were blank spaces in my memory. There were deep and sometimes illogical concerns about finances. There were far too many papers to deal with, too many important new problems to be solved, too many decisions to be made. I wished someone could take over for me, to work with the lawyer and accountant, to answer the daily mail, to do the shopping, to be there when my loneliness became unbearable.

Friends telephoned, offering invitations and assistance. "Let us pick you up," they said, "we'll go to the meeting together." I had to refuse. I could not accept this particular kindness. I was appreciative but I had to drive my own car, to be able to get away, to leave at my own time. Then I could meet my need to escape from one kind of loneliness to another. I learned how to put on what one woman called "my social mask"—a smile on my face that would hide the feelings beneath. Days passed in a blur. Evenings were better. They led to night, darkness and oblivion when I could sleep. Many times I made it through the day only because I knew night would finally come. I lived in the past and the present—with no expectation of a future.

The man was gone. So was the marriage. I mourned both. I was angry, not about his death, not about his dying, but for having to become his widow. For me, the label is a constant reminder of a tragic circumstance. A month after Jerry died, I had occasion to consult a new physician. I could not bring myself to check the "widow" box then, and I continue to ignore it wherever possible. Labels have always been abhorrent to me, that one in particular. I have come to terms with "single."

My daughter and her husband, who lived nearby, invited me to their home for dinner two or three times a week. We spent the evenings retelling old stories, discussing politics, books, business, friends, family—laughing when we could. Each of us was aware that life must go on despite the heavy overlay of grief we were experiencing. Their home was one place I could go and not be anxious to leave. But the leaving was terrible. I drove home weeping, even howling with grief. I was in pain. Literally, I was grief-stricken. It took two months before I could make it from their house to mine without bursting into tears.

A month later, I put myself back to work, volunteering where he and I had been involved before his illness required all our attention. I took on new responsibilities. I made plans to do things we could not because of his illness, or did not because they held no appeal for him. I made changes in the new house we had completed the previous October. I wondered if he would approve. I carried on our traditions, worried that I might fail him if I neglected any details. Then I realized I was allowing my memories of him to become restrictive. What I was doing and would do in the future could not in any way deny even a single moment of our thirty-four years together. "Lighten up," I told myself. "Get on with it!"

Mary Witt Wydman phoned me in March of 1989—a voice from the past after a hiatus of forty-two years. Getting in touch, a whim at the time, has turned out to be a great gift for both of us. Six months earlier, Mary had purchased a house in Santa Fe, New Mexico, where I live. Having read in the previous autumn issue of the *Smith Alumnae Quarterly* that our daughter had been married in our new home, she decided, she told me, to find out if we could revive what she remembered as a tenuous but cordial friendship. Her call had a remarkable effect on me. We are both sure that I recognized her voice. She was in town; we would have lunch. And, yes, we would find each other, no need for red carnations. The fact that Mary had not known me during my marriage gave me the opportunity to recall my earlier single self, to bring back a past identity that had included fairly successful career experiences. I believe the situation gave her an important recall opportunity as well. We began what has developed into a wonderful friendship, based on mutual past experiences but looking most often toward the future.

Throughout the summer, Mary and I discussed an idea that had been in my mind since Jerry's death. She developed a keen interest in the project I was proposing. We found our conversations more and more focused on it and its possibilities. She encouraged me to write to Smith College about the idea. "Go ahead, do it," she kept saying.

In September 1989, I wrote to Mary Maples Dunn, then President of Smith, suggesting a study of what happens when the unthinkable tragedy of a husband's death occurs. I explained that several of us, Smith alumnae and others, were discussing the enforced and traumatic changes we experienced. "Almost without exception," I wrote, "these women agree with me that too little has been done to prepare us for the life changes we will encounter after our husband dies. Men die younger than women, we know this, actuarially, even if, as married women, we don't want to think about it." Mary Dunn replied that the college was interested, and that I would hear from Nancy Steeper, Director of the Alumnae Association, "to discuss your idea."

I sent copies of my letter to our class secretary, asking her to forward them to the other class officers. Barbara Harrison Mulhern responded immediately. The concept Mary and I had in mind matched her conviction that more must be done to help married couples prepare for the eventuality of a death. She based her interest on her own experiences before and after her husband, Art, died in 1986. Barbara and I had lived in Comstock House at college, and, as with Mary, our relationship had been pleasant, but we had made little effort to keep in touch after graduation. We did enjoy meeting once at a pre-reunion

Alumnae College session many years ago. Now we would begin a new relationship—a project of sharing what happens to women when husbands die.

On August 28, 1990, Barbara, Mary and I met with Nancy Steeper at the college in Northampton, Massachusetts, to decide if there would be a first, practical step. Nancy mentioned that she had not experienced the death of any close family member. Consequently, much of what we had to say took her into new territory. At the end of a very long conference, we four committed to the project under the auspices—a somewhat vague connection—of the Alumnae Association. *When Husbands Die* would begin as soon as we could develop the questionnaire.

In the introduction to the questionnaire, I wrote that by the spring of 1991, I had moved past the second year of being single. Some aspects of my life, I noted, are better; some remain unhealed. "My sadness continues, as does my dislike of being so often alone. The most poignant reminders of Jerry's absence occur when there is something wonderful I would like to share with him, and it is diminished because I cannot."

I explained that every day, my faith, my family and my friends are helpful. I will always be grateful to our best friend, widowed several years before. She continues to be my guide. Carey, our black and white Cocker Spaniel, is my constant companion. She dispels the emptiness in my home, welcoming, protecting, amusing—and loving unconditionally. I find it interesting that her breeders named her "Carey, I'm a Survivor." Her demands are therapeutic for me. She has permitted me to retain a semblance of my past role as caretaker and provider. I continue to write about what is happening to me. I am beginning to look with some joy toward the possibilities of the future.

⇒ ⇒ ⇐ ⇐

Now years later, I am well and I am busy. I live in the same house that, much to my great good fortune, has become part of a two-house compound I share with my daughter, Elizabeth, and her husband. This has turned out to be a remarkably successful arrangement for all of us I am both delighted and relieved to be able to say. My little dog, Carey, is no longer with me. Elizabeth and Rob have a poodle and a cat whose care and company I share. More of my story is woven into the pages of this project as commentary and example. It has been impossible for me to put the material together without incorporating what I have experienced and learned since that early morning of February 9, 1989.

$$\backsim \quad \backsim \quad \backsim \quad \backsim$$

Barbara Harrison Mulhern, 1991

Let's face it: there is no way anyone can fully prepare herself or himself for what happens with the death of a spouse. The emotional trauma is far too strong. I think, however, that all of us who have been through it can identify certain experiences, people or events that helped to get us past the days of stunned shock, disbelief and grief.

At the time of Art's death, I felt fortunate that I had had a married lifetime of handling the household money. I knew about our investments, our retirement arrangements and how to prepare the income tax forms—partly because Art wanted me to and partly because, many years before, I had listened to a friend who was widowed in her thirties. She insisted that I prepare myself for the eventuality, at least on the subject of finances.

In the six weeks between Art's final diagnosis and his death, we were, with the help of a lawyer, able to review and simplify our legal affairs. I removed relevant documents from the safe deposit box, such as insurance policies, pension papers, Navy discharge papers, and anything else we knew would be needed to settle his affairs. We did not realize I would need the original of our marriage certificate to set up receipt of my widow's pension from Social Security.

Our daughter Pegeen was at our home the week before Art died. Our wise and caring oncologist made time to counsel her and to suggest some things that she should get me to do during the final days. Macabre as it may seem, he suggested that I read Tolstoy's *Death of Ivan Illyich*. He also insisted that I quietly make funeral arrangements and write Art's obituary before his death. I acted on and was glad for both suggestions.

I am still grateful to the doctor for his honesty. He did not pussyfoot about the prognosis and, when he knew the end would come sooner than he had first thought, he strongly urged that we move up the date of a planned family gathering. It was a bittersweet weekend for us all, with much laughter and many tears: one we will not forget.

My six children and their spouses were exemplary during Art's illness. Each found time to settle old disagreements, to share memories and old jokes, and to say good-bye. In spite of their own grief, their concern seemed to be for the two of us.

Living in a small town where everyone knows your business can be a plus. Even people who did not know me well cared about what was happening to us. The pats on the shoulder in the grocery store, the friendly hugs from Gary at the video rental shop meant more than the donors ever knew.

Neighbors, old friends, hospice volunteers and nurses, our good friend and priest all did many things to help me get through those early weeks, but much of my strength came from Art, himself. In the way of the Irish, he was never able to talk about his own death, even when it was imminent. He did, however, make it quite clear to me that I was not to look back, that I should look ahead and make a new beginning, a new life for myself.

Four years after Art's death, I took stock of Barbara Harrison Mulhern for the purpose of this story and this project. Those four years had been ones of enormous change and growth for me. I turned 61 just before Art died, and I realized that, given my heritage, I might have about twenty-five years of solitary living ahead of me. When I looked back from the vantage point of forty-eight months, I realized I had re-invented myself.

Originally, I alternated between the frenzy of getting things done at home and traveling to escape. I shed many, many tears alone, and many with family and friends in Colorado, Arizona, Dijon, Poitiers, Vermont, the United Kingdom and Cape Cod. We had a new athletic facility in our town, and I worked hard to get myself back into shape in aerobics classes, and alone, swimming solitary laps on Sundays and adding salty tears to the pool water. Public radio was my constant companion. I was almost fiercely independent, rejecting sincere offers of help, driving myself everywhere, I guess so I could escape at will.

Probably one of the best things I did was deliberately to seek new experiences and new friends. The summer after Art's death, I was a supernumerary in Britten's *A Midsummer Night's Dream*, a new me in a magical milieu. The following winter, with great trepidation, I signed up to go alone on a two-week European ski tour. At the last moment, I had cold feet and almost stayed home. Fortunately, I did go, and I had a great time. That experience gave me some very dear, new friends, as well as the self-confidence and incentive to get on with my life.

When I came home from the ski trip, I made the conscious decision to remain here in our town. I bought isolated hilltop property and began to make plans to build the wonderful, sunny house in which I now live. And, in the middle of the planning, I received a copy of Shirley's letter to Mary Dunn.

I had thought, often and long, about the financial experiences several of my friends and I shared after our husbands died. I spoke with people who, I believed, could work with me to begin a program that would assist women whose expertise in this field was slightly limited, or, sadly enough, completely lacking. I was astonished that so few people could understand what I had in mind. And, as I investigated further, I was amazed at how many women in my generation knew nothing about their finances, and how many men preferred the status quo of man/money, woman/household.

Of course I was interested in sharing stories! And if these stories could help our peers, more power to us! I traveled to Santa Fe to meet with Mary and Shirley. We renewed what ties we had and found many reasons for working together, especially if we were to create something that would help women prepare for the tragic inevitability we shared.

As for me, I continue to be alone a great deal, but never lonely. I have hawks and deer to watch, music to listen to, films to rent and books to read, as well as a rather large number of undone projects. I still travel often, with companions or by myself, but I am in pursuit of current interests. I no longer travel to escape. To bring my story up to the present, I continue to be deeply involved in my community and with my college. I have chosen my activities and friends with care, balancing the old with the new. I take joy in every day, good weather and bad. I know and welcome the beautiful animals whose land I share on our hilltop. New interests and new travels continue to bring new friends. I am often in touch with my children. They visit from time to time, and, in my camper, I drive to visit them, stopping along the way whenever there is something of interest to see. I am blessed with many grandchildren, so holidays are lively events, old traditions are strong, new traditions are ever developing.

I have come to the realization that I probably could not easily readjust my life to include a second marriage. I have become used to the freedoms that come with living alone, and I rather like them. Yes, I miss Art and the life we had together, but I am happy to have made peace with my single existence.

Eighteen years! Can it be that long since Art died? That is almost half of the thirty-seven years we had together. Grief is no longer the operative word: the word is gratitude, gratitude for the many wonderful memories of those years, gratitude for our six children, and gratitude for Art's last wishes for me to make a new life for myself.

I think of these last years as a coda, a coda balancing the prelude years before our marriage. In this time, I have been blessed with the chance to watch my children mature as they raise the thirteen grandchildren, and I have seen one become a grandmother, herself.

Travel has taken me as far as the sands of the Sahara, the rose-red ruins of Petra, and the Silk Road cities of Samarkind and Bokhara. A growing interest in the performing arts has brought me many wonderfully talented new friends. In addition, my love for skiing has changed my winters: I have spent the past six years as a professional ski instructor in Vermont.

Life goes on, varied and interesting. I pray for good health and a sound mind so that I can continue to enjoy each day. And may those whose grief is new and searing ultimately be as fortunate as I!

☞ ☞ ☜ ☜

Mary Witt Wydman, 1991

Bob Wydman died August 16, 1984, of lung cancer that metastasized to his brain Our daughter and I received a lot of support from the Cincinnati community where I have lived all my life, my parents and grandparents before me. We were also offered a lot of advice. Bob's planning had made the transition of financial change as painless as possible. We had, and still have, wonderful lawyers, wonderful friends. But there was the family business to consider.

The Witt Company had been in my family for almost one hundred years. The family men had always taken charge. I had been on the board; now I had controlling interest. Of course, I would sell. A good friend told me his free advice was worth its price, but because he felt he knew what Bob would have wanted, he advised me to put the company up for sale. It was the wrong advice. We laugh about it now. At the time, however, I did move on the idea of selling. Just before the papers were signed, I started to believe that I could run the Witt Company myself, with the help of all the staff. I could. I did. I am very proud of what we continue to accomplish.

My life since Bob's death has been all evolution, evaluation of my own strengths and weaknesses, and an assessment of my future. Much of what I did during the first year, I recognize only in retrospect. A new me, a future me, has evolved. I was fortunate to have the family business. It was and continues to be a wonderful way to expand my mind, my relationships—and my ego. The business has not solved the problem of being alone in a society where orientation to couples is the rule. I am very thankful to have my business involvement with both women and men. Life away from men is not fulfilling. Women need to hear men's voices, listen to their opinions, share ideas with them in business, on boards and in committees. It is often difficult for women who are alone to encounter men on these levels, to be able to work with them in positive, productive and non-threatening relationships. I might wish that men were more aware of this.

Shirley and I see each other often. With Barbara, the three of us have worked together for more than two years to further this project. There have been a lot of visits, phone calls and hours of conversation. The work has changed us, given us a broader understanding of this subject than we realized could happen. Although I was the first in our group of couples to experience this sudden singling, now many of my friends have endured the terminal illness or sudden death of their spouse and moved into another life style with me. My compassion for them is deeper than ever. So is my conviction that they can and will make new lives for themselves!

〜 〜 〜 〜

Now I have been single for twenty years. I travel often. I return every year to the place where Bob and I summered. I keep a wide circle of friends, new and old, and I am deeply concerned about each one of them. I am restless. I do not stay anywhere for very long. My interest in finding out what's happening in far away places has, for years, been very strong competition for any stay-at-home inclinations, but now there are two wonderful grandchildren who fill many happy hours, days and weeks, so I am at home more often—where the heart is. I continue to work out a schedule that accommodates all my interests. I try to plan almost two years ahead. I do not travel alone. I find friends wherever I go. My business commitments have changed. My daughter, Marcy, has become president of The Witt Company. I was chair of the board for several years, am now vice-chair. I continue to be involved with other boards and associations that interest me. I take more time for my family, my friends and myself.

When Bob died, I fiercely protected my name: Mrs. Robert Wydman. Sometime during these past years, I became, as well, Mary Wydman, a person in my own right, no longer dependent on my marital name for stability and safety. I am responsible for the "new Me,"—early on a frightening, but now a very exhilarating feeling—essential for the way I approach and will live the rest of my life.

2

⇒ The Project ⇐
Step by Step

After our meeting with Alumnae Director Nancy Steeper and the promise that the college was interested in the project, Mary, Barbara and I set about developing the questionnaire. In this document, we would share our own stories before we asked women for theirs—something of a *quid pro quo* that might help them overcome any reluctance. There was none. The response was gratifying and overwhelming.

The majority of the work fell to me. The idea was mine, I was the one of the three most recently experiencing the life changes, and I needed to do the work. As it happened, I soon slipped into the role of project writer, a responsibility that has been rewarding, difficult, heart-breaking, fascinating and, for me, vitally important.

I spoke often with Mary and Barbara, with a few scholars and other friends, with anyone else who wanted to talk about the project, and with my daughter and son, one an expert in discussion and organization, the other astonishingly adept with computers. Although the entire project became my main agenda, Mary and Barbara each developed agendas of particular interest to themselves. As she said in her story, Barbara had already done work on the financial problems women encounter. She had written material and presented it to a hospital in hopes the grief counselor would use it, but the doctors and staff showed no interest at all, so her commitment to a questionnaire section on finances was immediate. Mary's interest was more general. Mine lay in the areas of emotional recovery and how society reacted to me and, I must admit, how I reacted to it.

Our collaborative style set, the three of us began long conversations about the questions we would ask. We decided we would focus on six areas: grief and mourning, friends, health, society and societal relations, financial matters and reinvention of self. We checked local and national bookstores and any other sources we could find. I watched TV programs on topics that might relate to our subjects, but found them too deeply involved with the telling of single stories or rather light-hearted regarding the search for another husband. Nothing wrong with humor, but a bit too much fun relating how, having nursed the first husband, one becomes nurse, again, for the second. We checked computer listings. We also investigated public libraries. In mine in Santa Fe, I found more information on how to be beautiful-though-bereaved than how to survive. Of course, being beautiful has its good points. They were not ours at the time. During one of my return visits to Smith, I checked the college library. A dismal assortment tucked away in the lower stacks. Perhaps I should have looked under "Death" or "Dying," subjects of greater interest to young students, than under "Widow." During that search, I kept thinking that the young women who come to this college will grow up, many will be married and of these, most will be widowed. At some time, a woman's college needs to study its women!

An article announcing the project appeared in the *Smith Alumnae Quarterly*: "Coping with Widowhood Subject of Study." Anyone interested in receiving the questionnaire was to send her name and address to the Alumnae House in Northampton. The requests would be forwarded to me in Santa Fe. I would post the questionnaires and await their return. We also sent questionnaires, unsolicited, to several of Mary's friends who are widowed but did not attend Smith College. We had in mind using them as a control group. Eleven responded. Realizing that these women fit the demographics of the original group, we abandoned the control concept. Keeping the work entirely "Smith" was not vital to its readers or to its results.

During reunion in May 1991, at the invitation of the college, Mary, Barbara and I made a presentation for anyone interested in the project. Ours was one of several sessions scheduled the two days preceding graduation ceremonies. Responding to a very large turnout, we went well over our allotted time. Everyone attending had a story to share, a need to be heard. Women whose husbands were still living came to listen to what was being said, "to get prepared, just in case." News of what was happening reached Nancy Steeper and Mary Dunn. That evening, Mary and Nancy asked us to present a more complete session about our project the following year, at our own class reunion. Mary Dunn agreed to moderate this panel discussion.

The 1992 reunion discussion was very well attended. Again, some married women came to listen and learn. Women whose husbands had died came to listen, to learn, to share and, as some said, to heal. Sharing the stories, learning from each other, was uppermost in all our minds. We viewed this as proof of the continuing need to speak about the effect of events and the events themselves, to an audience anxious to hear. Some women admitted that they had not yet made out their wills. Some reported what happened because their husbands had not done this, either. Others were surprised that we had the temerity to think of doing the project. More said how much they approved the concept. One woman asked why we had not included a question about sex. Certainly we had discussed the subject, many, many times. But we decided not to move into this field. No one is naïve enough to pretend the subject is unimportant. Who wouldn't miss the pleasure and security of married sex! Who wouldn't be frustrated by the unwanted celibacy! The end of a marriage introduces myriad questions about sex, enough for several more projects, continually on-going. We chose to work with other changes in our lives. As it turned out, some women did share insights into the subject of sexuality, perhaps because we wrote at the end of the questionnaire, "if you wish to share other aspects of your story, please do so. We are very interested in what you have to say."

At the close of the panel discussion, several women asked for questionnaires. Word of mouth brought more requests. As of February 1999, the final count of questionnaires returned was 81 out of a possible 118. Two women asked that we not include their responses in the project. We have honored their requests for total privacy. Many women pointed out that they were helped through difficult times by the process of responding. One woman wrote, "Reflecting on all this hurts, but I'll do it and more if it helps."

From their class designations, we determined that our responders ranged in age from the mid-30s to the 80s. Thirty-two of the women were in college during the 1940s. By our calculations, the ages of these women, when they responded, were somewhere between the later 50s and the mid-60s. Seventeen were in the classes of the early 1950s, fifteen were in college in the 1930s, five in the 1960s, and three were in college in the 1970s, still young women. Before we completed this count, we had assumed it was statistically correct that women between the ages of 65 and 70 would be the ones left alone, widowed. We were surprised to learn this happened so often at a younger age. It happened to us, but we originally thought that was unusual. Mary was 59, Barbara 61, and I was 63. Some women in the project were widowed in their 30s.

At the time of their responses, seventeen women were in their first year of widowhood, seven in the second. Twenty-three had been widowed from three to five years, twenty-four from six to ten, and eight for more than ten years. Six women, who married again after the deaths of their first husbands, wrote about their first and their second bereavements.

Fifty-one women were well rooted in their communities when their husbands died. We assume many have remained. Twenty-four reported that they moved from their homes after their husband's death. Of those who gave us a time frame, nine moved within three to eighteen months, the others after several years. Advice to the bereaved always includes "Don't do anything in a hurry. Wait at least a year before making any changes." Apparently this advice is widely heeded. One woman, who moved soon after her husband died, said she needed the drama of change to help her carry on.

Of the women who worked during their married lives, forty-three were salaried and twenty-four were volunteers. Afterwards, of the forty-four who reported that they worked, twenty-one were salaried, twenty-three volunteered. Included among the professions: author, psychiatrist, teacher, priest, psychotherapist, sales representative, social worker, librarian—to mention a few. Many others held management positions. Volunteering included board memberships, tutoring, community assistance, and the myriad aspects of helping that always appear under the category. A great number of responses indicated how important it is to become and stay busy as grief work continues. From these, we deduced that many women were involved outside the home even though they did not say so. Obviously, the women with young children were busy beyond belief. They had little time to meet the needs of their own grieving.

The majority of our responders enjoy some degree of financial security. When we presented our idea to the college, we realized we would be dealing with less than a norm concerning this subject. One woman wrote, "Judging from your three stories, and the questions, there is an assumption that there will be no real money problems for Smith graduates of our age. No doubt that is largely true. But there are cases like mine, when we had to live for several years on my meager salary and were on the edge near the end, and deeply worried about possible enormous medical bills to come. As it happened, the financial problems cleared up, and I was even able to retire when I wanted to.

Others may not have been so fortunate." Her observation is important. In the questionnaire we did not ask for financial specifics. However, we strongly believe that no matter what the financial picture, finances and how to handle them are one of the major problems that confront women who are suddenly left alone.

Reviewing the enormous amount of material the returned questionnaires represented, and deciding how to manage it for optimum effectiveness became my primary and most difficult task. Difficult because every story started with tragedy, and I was still in the midst of my own. Fascinating because there was so much to learn, so much strength, so much courage—and so much love. I asked Kay Halpern, a friend and scholar, to work with me. Kay's field was sociology. She had close ties to the Smith College School of Social Work through her Boston University and professional connections. And she was a widow.

Kay and I quickly realized that women are the real heroes of these stories even though, in most cases, the valor of their husbands is their major theme. During his illness, my own husband was brave and courageous, willing to go through trial treatments to help both himself and the research being done at Mayo Clinic. Towards the end, he had to accept rejection for new treatment because he had already experienced enough chemicals to make continued medical applications extremely dangerous and not scientifically valuable. We knew this might happen. From the beginning, and while we were still very hopeful, Jerry and I traveled halfway across the country every six weeks so he could receive chemotherapy. He did not handle the nausea well. Hair loss, the first time, was bothersome but not traumatic. The second, third and fourth times, it was unimportant. His most difficult moments came, he said, when dear friends showed how much they cared for him. He felt he could not respond adequately. Tears flowed. Jerry was attuned to giving help, not receiving it.

I have heard there is a saying about the death of a spouse that suggests the one who lives on is the one who loved most. Although this implies a contest, which is unthinkable, it is also an attempt to express our human inadequacy in dealing with the "why" of the situation. Many friends admit that they believe their husbands could not have survived the trauma of widower-hood. Everyone has heard stories of men who died soon after their wives. Whether any of this speaks to the truth is questionable. Here you take your choice, as you do with much that is said about who grieves and how the process works.

At the beginning of the questionnaire, we stated that our purpose was to uncover common threads that have helped each of us survive the initial throes of widowhood and forge new lives for ourselves. The specifics of each person, each marriage, and each family are different. Our ways of handling problems differ as much as we do. Perhaps, however, there are some common experiences and tools that we can pass on to others to help them prepare for this unwanted transition from married to single, and to help and affirm those of us who are still reinventing ourselves. During this process, we added, "The project will not use names of responders or their families, or geographical references such as address or community."

Those who participated in the project, including the three of us, took a risk. The responders by giving us access to their stories, we by assuming the project eventually would reach a helpful conclusion. We also put the questionnaire at risk by starting with a very tough question, a very simple one: "What happened?" Too difficult? Would people be willing to give us their stories, to go over it all, again?

Actually, most of the questionnaires came back with answers that filled every possible part of the pages, accompanied by letters telling us more about the stories. The responses also offered opinions about the work we had begun, many with thanks that the project was being attempted. A few wondered, as we did, what would happen once the project was completed.

The women whose stories fill the following pages are, for the most part, wonderfully resilient and very strong. They are aware of their vulnerability. They are willing to work hard to reorient and reinvent themselves as they make a new life that will include joy, independence, productivity and satisfaction during the twenty, thirty or however many years ahead of them. In our own cases, Barbara, Mary and I figure on a few more than twenty years, actuarially speaking, that we will live after the deaths of our husbands. Along with many of the others involved in the project, we expect that we will do it independent of another marriage.

3

☞ Grief and Mourning ☜
Tell Us What Happened

From our own experiences, Barbara, Mary and I knew it would be helpful for many women to have an opportunity to relate what happened to their husbands while, perhaps for the first time, wholly in control of the story telling. This might be a time for total sharing, an experience with no interruptions, no worries about making a listener sad or uncomfortable. A time for catharsis, for healing. Would the responses differ depending on the length of time since the husband's death? And, very important, would the question demand more of the responders than they were willing to disclose?

The returns showed us that women did want to tell their stories. They had as much to say ten years later as the women whose husbands died a year ago, two years ago, three to five, or six to ten.

A common thread. The need to tell the story does not diminish with time, particularly if we are permitted to do so without restrictions and in a sense, privately, but assured of an interested "listener." I have not found anyone truly willing to hear my story. Is it too personal, too painful or too lengthy? I tried once, with a very dear friend who is almost as given to the spoken word as I. She had her own story she wanted to tell, so we exchanged roles and I became her listener.

During the first three years, I made my own notes, lengthy ones, and kept duplicates of letters I wrote to friends. As I reread these pages, I find they are a sad history of a very sad time when, despite a lot of activity, work and traveling, I was still vulnerable, still lonely, still filled with deep sorrow. I realize that I used my computer keyboard as a kind of crying towel.

With the passage of time, I no longer dwell on the minute by minute events of my husband's final struggle. I was told these memories would become less vivid. I am not sure this is true, but I know they do not come to mind as often as they did during the first two years. I certainly remember the end of his life, the hospice nurse coming, the undertakers arriving and leaving, and the beginnings, again, of the awful emptiness that is all too familiar once you have experienced the death of a person you have lived with and loved. What I cannot bring to mind are the events of the week following the memorial service. My memory is blank. My sister stayed with me; I am sure our friends were wonderful. Exhaustion and grief are all I remember.

The day Jerry died, in addition to calling relatives, we phoned back east to a priest, a good friend who knew us when our children were young. He expressed his sorrow, then told us to sit down with our picture albums and a bottle of brandy. "Indulge yourselves with memories and love," he said. I do not like brandy. I do like his advice. We also called the priest who had been rector of our local church and had moved on to another parish. Unable to change his schedule so he could attend Jerry's memorial, he insisted we not delay, saying, "After the service is when you get on with life."

Before the project began, I expected that most men would live until the age of 70. That did not happen to Art, Bob or Jerry. They were all younger. From the responses, statistics in this regard are startling. Some men died in their 30s and 40s. Seventeen died in their 60s. Of these, one died at 60, two were only 61, two were 62, four died at 64, two at 67, two at 68, and four at 69, including my husband. Of those who died in their 50s, one was just 50, two were 52, one 53, three were 55, five 57, one was 58, and five were 59. Although eighteen husbands died in their 70s, four in their 80s, and one at 92, of the deaths reported, forty-two happened before age 70. They show the tragic truth that the assumed three score years and ten is a goal not often achieved.

Are these statistics important as demographics of a larger group? I suspect there is truth in what we found. Cancer and heart attacks caused the majority of deaths—twenty-two cancer deaths, nineteen deaths from heart conditions, including heart attacks. Other causes include three from massive strokes, three from aneurysms, three from brain tumors, two from pneumonia, and one each from renal failure, rare blood disorder, chronic pulmonary disease, viral infection, pancreatitus, emphysema, Alzheimer's, Parkinson's, flu, ALS, anaphylactic shock from a bee sting, internal bleeding and Hodgkin's disease. There were several fatal injuries. One woman said her husband's death was caused by poor medical judgment. Two others blamed the deaths on faulty medical procedures. There were five decisions not to continue life support. Responses indicated that twenty-eight husbands died in hospital, twenty-four at home, four in hospice centers and four in nursing homes.

The majority of the husbands were already suffering from serious illnesses diagnosed at least a year before they died. A third of the men died suddenly, without indication of previous illness. Heart attacks, accidents or misdiagnoses were the causes of these deaths. Several women wrote that they and their children were "with him" when he died, certainly a situation to be desired. I spoke with a friend who had not been present at her husband's death. She admitted she felt "a kind of guilt" about this. How could she know he would die at that specific moment? She had been with him in the hospital every day for weeks. Hadn't she been faithful enough?

⇜ ⇜ ⇜ ⇜

Our question asking what happened also asked if the death was expected. Many women said, and I believe, the answer is "no." Even if the illness is severe or acute, and warning of imminent death given, no one expects death to occur when it does. Life and hope exist together. Hope is never extinguished until the instant of death. And who knows when that moment will be? Women whose husbands die unexpectedly say this sudden death is terribly hard to survive. Death with a known illness is also terribly difficult. In terminal illness, the element of surprise is less, but the physical strain of watching and waiting is very great. Does advance notice help? Is the tending and watching more difficult than the instant discovery? Is it worse to make a NOCODE (hospital instructions: do not resuscitate) decision? Who knows? This is a one-time experience. It happens differently for everyone. One woman said of her husband, "He died suddenly, unexpectedly. Overweight and in medium health, death seemed a possibility, but a few more years 'down the road.'" Another, "We knew his end was near but kept on, lived on borrowed time and amazed all doctors. Yes I expected his death, but not when he last landed in the hospital and died within three days." Other women wrote: "His going was terribly unexpected although he had been ill with multiple myeloma for three and a half years. Death is always unexpected, really." "His death, in three days, of pneumonia, was, of course, not unexpected but not anticipated so soon." "Of course the death wasn't really unexpected, its imminence was just denied." "I expected him to die and had thought about it, but not that day." "Is death expected? Well, yes and yet no. Until it comes, there is hope of sorts and when it comes it is a terrible jolt!"

Certainly a sense of relief is unique to a lengthy, terminal illness. Guilt, bitterness, recrimination, wishes that it had happened differently—these result from any death. So do understanding and acceptance. However, according to our responders, understanding and acceptance usually occur somewhere down the road. If the need to deny the coming of death is acute, much more so is the wish to deny it has happened. But it has. And we must search for signs, words, emotions and symbols to help us deal with what has now become a new and unwanted reality.

The day before Jerry McNally died, our son-in-law brought us several pots of daffodils, February's spring sign. I put them in the living room near a very wide window that looks east to New Mexico's Sangre de Cristo Mountains. That morning, Jerry had moved from our bedroom into the guestroom. In the afternoon, our daughter, her husband and our son came to stay at our house. Jerry's struggles began around midnight. He died two hours later. Some time after three in the morning, when the undertakers and hospice nurse had left, we tried to sleep wherever we could be comfortable. I lay down on the living room sofa. When first light awakened me, I looked at the daffodils framing the beautiful morning sky, and I used everything I could think of to help me face the day. There was the hymn, "Morning Has Broken, Like the First Morning." There were the mountains, "I will lift up my eyes to the hills; from where is my help to come?" There was the "host of golden daffodils." To this day, daffodils remind me vividly of regeneration. They are my signs and symbols. I have a young friend whose husband died, as Jerry did, on February 9, but just a few years ago. Several times I brought her daffodils on that date, and will again this year. They help both of us. The message? Use everything you can to help you move ahead. Be open to what is around you. Find your own daffodils. Cherish them.

꙰ ꙰ ꙰ ꙰

I have already mentioned that the project originated as an idea during the year in which Jerry died—the first year of my widowhood. Just before I began the second year, I was told by a friend that what was to come would be different and very difficult. It was. Having lived through the pain and anguish of the first year, I now had to do it again, lonely anniversary by anniversary, holiday by holiday, Sunday by Sunday. But this time I knew what to expect and what I had to accept. I would have to do more than survive; I would have to prevail. By the third year, I was growing stronger, and the project was in full swing. I sent out and received more and more questionnaires, recording the responses in my computer. I began to think seriously about how to structure this wonderful material so it would offer the most help to the people we wanted to reach. Share the stories; report similarities, differences and common threads; help the readers discover, for themselves, the pathways that lead to regeneration. This was what we wanted to do. If time heals all wounds, or is supposed to, then time is our ally. I already knew about the first year, and the second. Now I was going—and growing—through the third. We set up our own time line: first year, second year, third to fifth, sixth to tenth, ten or more years following the husband's death. The first year holds trauma unlike any other. The second year is a time of learning hard lessons, facing harsh realities, understanding that you, alone, are responsible for the life change you must accept, the new life you must develop. During the third, fourth and fifth years, life gets better, handling difficult situations becomes easier but everything is not resolved. Is it ever? After five years, growth can be remarkable; after ten years, as one woman said, "I seldom think about myself as anyone other than who I am today." But asked to remember, almost everyone, regardless of time, reveals strong feelings and tells poignant stories. They say that the stories of widowhood should become better known, increasing understanding of what happens when husbands die, and helping those who will have to learn for themselves.

The first section of the questionnaire, Grief and Mourning, begins with "What Happened?" and moves on to related subjects. In addition to sharing how their husbands died, responders were asked the following. In what ways were memorial services helpful to you?

Which parts of the grief process stand out most vividly in your memory? What kinds of help and support did you welcome during the early stages of your grief? Later? What spiritual resources did you lean on in the early stages? Later?

〜 〜 〜 〜

Helen's Story (First year)

Helen answered the questionnaire the same year that her husband, Alan, died. She was in her early 50s when his death occurred. He was 53. They had lived in the same community for six years and were actively involved. He was employed by a university in a mid-sized city; she worked "sporadically, teaching and later, floral arranging." They had two grown children who lived away from their parents' home area. Helen writes that she and Alan had been married twenty-six years when he was diagnosed with a brain tumor. The tumor affected his left side motor control. The doctors were honest with her, she said. They explained the wide range of expectancy for this particular situation as shown in a history of statistics. "Knowing all the possibilities, I lived with each of them constantly." In three months time, her husband was bedridden. With the help of hospice he remained comfortably at home for another six months. Then he slipped into a coma. Helen said that even though their two children did not live close by, they came often during their father's illness. They and the rest of his family came quickly to be with him during the last hospitalization. Although he was in a comatose state, many people who had visited came again, this time to say goodbye to their beloved friend. Alan died in early March.

Helen wrote that the religious service was guided and led by loyal friends and clergy who had remained by their side during her husband's illness. "Their reflections on him and our family raised our self-esteem, fallen in the face of defeat." She continued, "We were able to recapture the personality of father, husband, friend and companion as it was before he became ill. Children, family and friends discovered new memories about this loving person as they listened to events others shared. Familiar stories brought him back to us. The sharing of grief with hundreds of loving people was uplifting, providing a safety valve for so many deep emotions.

"My grief was extreme during those first two months. I allowed myself to shed tears. I talked about the pain with friends who openly shared their own tears and grief. I am grateful that I did not have to shield my feelings from friends. Our friends and I did not allow our grief to separate us. My own private anguish and the extreme depths of my loneliness were excruciating, greater then I could ever have imagined. I felt lost. I floundered in a wilderness. Early mornings, the first awakenings, were terrible. Three weeks later, evenings were worse. Then nighttime. I could not sleep."

Asked which parts of the grief process stand out most vividly in her memory, Helen responded: "The first month especially and the second month, when I allowed myself to shed more tears and talk about the pain with many of the staff where he had worked. I was totally unprepared for the many friends who openly shared their tears and grief with me. Again, it was a relief not to have to shield my feelings. No amount of preparation could have prevented or protected me from the grief I experienced. At times I felt myself floundering in a wilderness that had never before been known to me."

About the help and support she received at first and then later, Helen wrote, "Family members and friends would call in the evening. We had lengthy conversations that allowed me to vent many of my feelings. Outings for lunch or dinner helped to take up some of the slack, particularly in the evenings when the loneliness was grueling. Some four months later," Helen continued, "the people who helped me complete the necessary move from company housing were wonderful. Men friends offered to mow the large lawns, one shared financial information—greatly appreciated!" The children had been "sterling," she added. Her response indicated that they helped throughout their father's illness and were very close to her, calling many times to see how she was, offering her encouragement. "Instead of me being burdened with concern for their well being, they were concerned with mine." Her sister stayed with her for a week following the burial. Her sister-in-law phoned frequently and regularly sent cards with supportive messages. Helen made a note on the questionnaire about cards and letters that arrived every day, poignant personal notes, "sharing grief, love and concern." Alan's parents called weekly. "I have been blessed," she wrote. "Blessed to have so much emotional support. I can say that none of my family members shut me out because their own grief was so strong." Helen added, "Weekly mass was a comfort. But in the spring it was difficult to get through the Passion and Easter Gospels. I wanted Alan there with me. Not risen, not somewhere else. The religious laity who were so much a part of our lives during the illness always included me in their church events. These services and meetings were the only places on campus where I knew I would be included in events on a regular basis. I never had a moment's concern about being welcome or being only one-half of what had been a wonderful whole. We were all healing."

Jane's Story (First year)

Jane's story differs from Helen's in several respects even though they both were experiencing the first year of widowhood. Jane's husband, John, was 71 when he died. Judging from her class designation, she was about the same age. John was a minister. They had been married for forty-nine years, had three children and six grandchildren, all of whom lived far away. During their marriage, Jane had worked briefly, teaching nursing. They had retired and, because of John's condition, moved into a care community. After John died, Jane began volunteer work. Here's what she shares with us.

"After a year of alternate mini-strokes and G-I bleeding, John had a more severe stroke which necessitated a move from the hospital to a nursing home. His condition deteriorated progressively, visibly, and he died of internal bleeding. His death was a blessed relief for him.

"Since he was a minister, he had strong convictions about funeral services. He had outlined the kind and content of the memorial service he wanted for himself. The music was to be his favorite, pertinent selections. The message was derived from his own statements and faith connections, delivered under happier circumstances." Writing about the process of grieving, Jane says, "There was no anger, no denial. I thought I was under great control, but a sudden word, hymn, letter of condolence would touch an inner switch and open the tear ducts—brief but unexpected episodes which occur less frequently now, four months later." Asked about help and support, she says she welcomed being able to speak honestly and freely to family and friends about how she felt at any particular time, right from the beginning. "And I still do!" Spiritual resources? "My church community is very supportive, church services and music are very sustaining. I rely on words like these: 'All things work together for good to them who are called according to His purposes' and 'It is given to love to keep its own through all eternity.'"

Responses to the questionnaire often advise women to "get busy" as part of the healing process. In the context of Grief and Mourning, can one ask if funeral rites serve, secondarily—or in some cases, primarily—to keep the bereaved busy? The few days before and the day of a service (traditional or not) bring great busy-ness. Phoning, gathering, greeting, making decisions, feeding, attending, even searching for the correct clothes as our mothers searched for the right black hat. One woman noted that she intentionally wore white "as an instinctively felt symbol of my desire to celebrate his life, his contributions, his witness, his hope in Christ." Does this necessary period of intensity move us away from despair or keep despair at bay? We take charge of the event, if we can, and, with help, we create a community that sustains us, keeps us occupied, before we plunge into lonely grieving. Are we, in a sense, rescued by the physical requirements of this time?

Every culture calls for specific family and community reactions to a death. What happens may differ, but, in every case, something happens. In our society, these happenings involve disposition of the body, ceremony, visiting, gifts of food, offers of financial assistance, letters, phone calls, offers of help—a deluge of kindness that shows caring and love. Dealing with these is not easy. One or two women said they needed to be alone; they could not handle the work. For those who carried on, did the work keep them from sinking under the weight of their grief? Were traditions helpful? Were the women too busy to think anywhere but in the present? I hope so. These events give us a specific part to play. We are preparing for and sharing in a celebration of his life. The reality of the situation, the emptiness to come, can be put off for this honoring and solemnity. Isn't the next day time enough to begin life as a widow?

Two women wrote of their interest in earlier traditions of ceremony and mourning now left behind by our present practices and our culture. One wondered if there should be a widow's ring; the other said much is still to be desired concerning how women are treated today. We did question whether the well-defined Victorian role of widowhood might have brought some relief from what became, fairly often, a need to explain ourselves and our situation. Wearing black, then gray, then lavender could send a signal, provided other people knew what the colors meant. Do men still wear black armbands? When does the term widow—one I thoroughly dislike— become operational? Was I the widow to the florist? The clergy? The funeral home? I have no recollection of anyone using the term during those first days. I know I would have been upset had it been said in my presence.

The questions we asked about funeral, memorial or any other services came from our conviction that closure is the needed concept.

Closure for whom and of what finality may be open to discussion, but most people believe that something needs to be done to mark his death—and his life. As one woman wrote, "A sentence needs a period at the end of it. A sonnet must have a last line. We need to say a ritual 'Good-bye.'"

Although four women said that no services were held, and seven were negative about receiving any solace, others who indicated they did not have services did gather friends and family in special places where words were said. Certainly, for them these were wonderful kinds of services, memorials in the best sense, ceremonies of closure.

For many, services in synagogue or church are "what we do." A few women indicated they did what their husbands would expect them to do. Eight reported that they and their husbands had planned the service, together.

Responders who specified their religious affiliations were from Catholic, Christian Science, Episcopal, Jewish, Lutheran, Methodist and Presbyterian communities. While the majority of these women found the services helpful, several added that it was "the doing" that was the greatest help. Again and again, the presence of family and friends was most important. "Although the service did not mean much to me, the presence of our friends was a great comfort." The importance of this presence is a common thread running throughout the responses. In a formal service, filled pews indicate respect, love, friendship, sorrow, sympathy and caring. I have attended a lot of memorial services since Jerry's. I am in the aging group; more friends are dying. Earlier I might have found excuses to stay away from a funeral or memorial. Now I go in hopes that my being there will add even the smallest amount of help. Presence is a gift anyone can give.

While the number of people who attended the service was important to many, others wanted only a few close friends or just the family. Most of the responders spoke of formal religious services, but everyone who mentioned gatherings said that these gave family and friends opportunity to take part in some kind of closure. A ceremony sanctioned by a trusted organization, one that is usually traditional and predictable, a small gathering held out of doors in a beautiful setting, a journey to spread his ashes, even a dinner party—all these were mentioned. For everyone, "our own way" is best. A judgment call would be impossible and unwarranted.

In our case, there was a church service because church is central to who we are. Within hours of Jerry's death, our daughter and I had met with the Episcopal priest and the organist, made necessary arrangements, selected readings and music for the traditional service. We chose a prelude I had hoped would be played at Elizabeth's wedding the previous October, but Jerry's illness had precluded anything other than a very small, simple ceremony at home attended by seven of us and our dogs. (One of the Cocker Spaniels could not understand why the minister didn't want to play ball with her during the ceremony.) At the memorial service, our daughter and son read from scripture; clergy from three churches took part—good friends, one a woman who had helped us during the difficult days. I am thrilled to report that the rector permitted this woman priest to preside at the Communion Service, a first for the particular church to which we belonged at the time. The Women's Guild of the church handled a reception for the hundreds of people who attended the funeral. This was a kindness for which I will always be grateful.

Jerry and I did not plan a service in advance. That it would occur required no discussion. As I recall, it was difficult for him, years before, to agree that cremation would happen for each of us. Burial was never discussed. Both of us knew we should fill out the church's service-intent form. We never got around to it. Nor have I done it yet.

The practicality of filling out a service-intent form is obvious, even if seldom acted on. It may be that most church people are unaware the forms exist or, more likely, even if aware, they are sure they can do this task "another day." As someone said, "At least, talk to each other about it."

On the advice of a priest and unknown to me at the time, our daughter and her husband visited the funeral home a few days before her father died. The point was notification of a possible death and indication that we would need the mortuary's services. Because of this preplanning, even though they were called at two-o'clock in the morning, the mortuary sent its ambulance within the hour. Although we hated what was happening, we were impressed with their kindness and efficiency. The early visit and planning also resulted in a financial saving. The hospice nurse, who was called immediately after Jerry died, was remarkably caring. She came as quickly as she could, signed the death certificate, and sat with us until his body was removed.

I wanted to write Jerry's obituary and did so with Elizabeth's assistance. We took the article to the local paper. I submitted it directly to *The New York Times*. A mistake. Sunday publication was delayed until Monday because the newspaper needed to determine, through the mortuary, that Jerry had died. This is accepted practice, for good reason. The mortuary would have been pleased to send the notice, but at the time, I wasn't able to listen to their offerings. Even that single visit to the funeral home was torture, a part of a reality I did not want to face.

I learned that urns or boxes of certain dimensions are required for our church columbarium. The container we chose, with his remains—not "cremains," please—would have to be picked up, held somewhere and later placed at the church. The "who, how and when" of the process meant additional decisions. Jerry's ashes are still in the church columbarium. I do not intend that they stay there. I have yet to decide the next step. Not a mountain top, although our home looks out on two beautiful mountain ranges. Not Alaska where we worked, on and off, for many happy years. Jerry didn't like cold. Not the sea. After five World War II years in the Pacific, this Iowa-bred officer who never liked to swim had enough of water and watery graves. Perhaps, like one or two others in the project, I will let time pass until what remains of us can be scattered together. I should decide where, put the instructions in my will or at least inform my children. And I should do it soon.

⁓ ⁓ ⁓ ⁓

Caroline's Story (First year)

Caroline also was in the first year when she joined the project. She and her husband, Donald, had been married forty-one years. An attorney, he was 72 when he died. They had three married children, two young grandchildren, all living far away. Caroline and Donald had to deal with a lengthy illness and a long nursing home experience. He had a history of heart problems, and in the last three years before his death, he had a second by-pass operation and three other hospitalizations. "Following a cardiac rehab session," Caroline wrote, " he collapsed and lost oxygen to the brain. He was in a coma for two and a half weeks, and not expected to recover. However, he did, but with very serious short-term memory loss. For the last two years, I ran both our lives completely. At the end, I could not manage, and had to put him in a nursing home. There, after three months of gradual decline, Donald died."

In addition to her responses to our questions, Caroline wrote a letter, part of which tells about their experiences while Donald was in the nursing home.

"Dear Shirley: At last I've completed your questionnaire. I enjoyed the panel at reunion. It made me rather weepy, but listening to others is good for one, and enlightening. We can't help each other too much with the emotional aspects of death, but we can share! I hope the project goes along well. It's a wonderful way to help people in their grieving process and to let them know they are not alone. I, myself, will have to see what comes next. I'm relishing having a lot of time and don't feel I have to rush out and accomplish something. The summer is filled with children's visits, the cottage and golf. When fall comes, maybe all the extra time and loneliness will loom too large. Who knows? I'm not planning anything at the moment.

"One aspect I would like to comment on. When Donald went into the nursing home the last three months, to his friends it was as if he was gone. No one sent cards or letters; no one sent flowers or plants. When he was in the hospital, on the other hand, he was showered with attention, and even I received many, many cards. This time, nothing.

"Are people afraid because they know it's terminal? It would have been nice for him and for me to have some flowers around and cards to pin up. Friends realized that his mind was pretty much gone, but he could have had something to look at. In retrospect, I think about this and wonder. At one point, a friend said she wished she could do something for him. I said send some flowers, and so she did. That was one exception. As for visits, I did discourage them because he could not carry on a conversation. He would know anyone who came but could initiate no talking. A few close friends came a few times, anyway. I was grateful for that. It was a lesson for me. People in nursing homes are still with us, even if not too alert, and their families would feel someone was thinking of them. Stays in nursing homes are obviously a lot longer than stays in hospitals, so it seems attention is needed more than ever. So, as I say, I learned something."

About the memorial service for her husband, Caroline said, "Our three children and I talked to our minister to plan the service. It was very interesting and helpful to me to hear what each child said about their father. The service itself was fine; the minister gave an exceptionally fine eulogy.

"So much of the grieving and sadness preceded Donald's death," Caroline continued, "because one could see the decline, especially mentally, over several years. He had been so very bright! I had to endure this day by day. He knew there was something wrong and it was very frustrating for him. And, of course, I could not help. The best support was the Respite Center where he went three days a week, because the people there understood problems like his, and I could talk to them." Caroline did not respond to the question of spiritual support.

⇒ ⇒ ⇐ ⇐

The next chapters follow the stories of Helen, Jane and Caroline, and of several other women who wrote, in similar detail, about their experiences from their perspectives as widows in the second year, third to fifth, sixth to tenth or more than ten years of widowhood. Their stories of "what happened" are in this chapter. Later, along with Helen, Jane and Caroline, they share their responses to questions about their families, their friends, their health, their finances, their return to society and their reinvention of themselves.

⇒ ⇒ ⇐ ⇐

Pat's Story (Second year)

Pat's husband, Peter, died the year before she became part of the project. She is writing about her experiences as a widow in the second year. They had been married thirty-eight years. He was 64; she was younger. There were four children and three grandchildren, all of whom lived far away from the community to which Pat and Peter recently had come. Pat worked as a teacher during their marriage and after his death. She enclosed a note with her questionnaire, saying, "This was more difficult than I had anticipated, rousing memories and emotions that I wasn't prepared for. However, I'm glad to have had the opportunity to share. In the long run, the exercise has proven very therapeutic."

Pat begins her story as follows. "Peter was diagnosed with lung cancer two years ago. Last year he died, a paraplegic with a tumor on his spinal cord. Following unsuccessful radiation treatments, he had come home to live another ten days. Our eldest daughter and I were his primary caregivers—exhausting work but important to us.

"While Peter was hospitalized, we planned his funeral service, selecting his favorite hymns, the readings, etc., and our children added their choices. The involvement made us confident we were doing what Peter wanted. But even more, we had a sense of his participation. Following the cremation, all of us, children and grandchildren, flew to our favorite country area and spread his ashes over his beloved hills and lake. It gave us a sense of a task well done."

Pat's most vivid memories of grief? "My vulnerability without my closest friend and confidante," she wrote, "plus quirky things. The shape of a head in a car passing mine would reduce me to tears. It wasn't Peter, couldn't be, but perhaps?" What kinds of help and support did you receive and welcome? "Peter and I had moved here only two years before his illness, so there were no long-term ties with local people. However, church members and neighbors poured out emotional and practical support. It was hard for me to accept help, harder still to ask for it. After all, I was superwoman and my grief was so intense and so private! My earlier counselors developed problems of their own, and I tried counseling them. I was extremely uneasy socially for several months, but now enjoy limited socializing. The unexpected call or last minute plan is still more appealing." As for spiritual resources, Pat had many. "Our acting rector was an unusually perceptive and empathetic person—and a woman. She was a tireless resource, and my husband was as devoted to her as I, both as friend and spiritual guide. Since Peter's death I have attended two church sponsored weekends: a retreat for bereaved spouses and a Cursillo weekend. Both generated strong bonding as well as spiritual support, particularly the Cursillo (a 'Small Course in Christianity') since it is an on-going involvement."

Were family members supportive? "Our children have been extraordinary. Throughout this experience they have kept in regular contact and have made my recovery 'easier'—that's probably the worst word—because of their support. Looking back now, I am aware of how much I took from them, and how little I have been able to respond to their needs. Members of my family and my in-laws have been and continue to be strongly supportive. I am the first to lose a spouse, so their attentions are often awkward or inappropriate, but they are responding!"

⤟ ⤟ ⤞ ⤞

Eight other women wrote that they, too, were the first widows in their immediate group—a difficult situation made more difficult. I was fortunate to have the guidance of an older, dear friend whose husband had died several years before. The three of us had spent a lot of time together until Jerry's illness became incapacitating. We belonged to the same church; we liked each other's politics; we delighted in living in Santa Fe. She gave good advice, listened well and often spoke about Jerry and her husband, Al, whom I had met only once. Similarly to Pat, she often "saw" Al in the early days, and said I would probably see Jerry. I wondered if I would hear his footsteps or feel his presence. I never saw him. I did dream about him, and I felt his presence several times. My mentor warned me that the part of our lives together I would miss the most were the opportunities we had to touch and be touched. Not sexual intimacy, she said, as much as the intimacy of closeness we had developed over the years: the way we held each other's hands, the way we greeted each other with a kiss, the way he touched my shoulder when he walked past my chair—our gestures of marriage. She was emphatic about the need to touch and be touched. "Get your hair done," she said, "have a manicure, get a massage, hug others, let them hug you, shake hands with people, let a friend help you up the stairs. Do everything you can to recognize and satisfy the human need to be close."

⤟ ⤟ ⤞ ⤞

In responding to the questionnaire, not every woman wrote at length nor did every woman share experiences based on every question. A few found several questions not applicable, used simple negatives or left the spaces blank. The vast majority, however, did answer fully, particularly the earlier questions about grief, mourning, family and friends. Responders who are in the third and fourth categories of the project—widowed from three to five years or six to ten—greatly outnumber the women in earlier and later groups. When these women responded to the question of grieving, they showed that memories are strong. Loneliness still exists for most but it has become less acute and less constant. A few in these two groups say they still have trouble dealing with their grief and believe this situation will continue: "I still experience terrible attacks of fear and deep sadness." "I was not aware of a grief process, only of an unchanging sorrow that he was gone. I still feel that same kind of sadness after five years have passed." "The unreality of my life, now and since then. I function on one level, can never really satisfy a deeper level. I am happy on the surface in some, in fact, many ways, but I am deeply unhappy in a basic way. The nearly seven years have proved this to me." The wounds of widowhood are very slow to heal. They leave deep scars. Although most women discovered or developed ways of coping with their futures, making them interesting, fun, rich and rewarding, they admit that the scars remain.

Somewhere I came across a saying about how we move along: "It will never get well, but it will get better." Not positive, but understandable. "It will never be forgotten" is a fair addition. The death of a beloved person is never an isolated incident. People who have not experienced the loss cannot contemplate the shocking emptiness, the absence that is constantly remembered, continually evidenced. When a child, a parent, a great friend dies, there is incredible grief. There is pain, pain that truly hurts, pure physical pain. There are emotional swings, disorientation, guilt, anger and loneliness. When a spouse dies, the widow, forced into a life change, grieves for her former life, for herself, for what she had to leave behind, and for what will be ahead. Some work through their grief more quickly than others. Does it take two years? Three years? Five? Everyone's calendar differs. Although we did not pose a direct question, we believe the shared stories indicate that women must work through three to five years of grief and change before they feel well on their way to a recovered, reinvented life. The hard work of grieving must be accomplished before healing takes place. Healing is never oblivion.

〜 〜 〜 〜

Those women who have remarried—six responded to the questionnaire—shared stories equally complete, sad and self-searching, so we cannot say that remarriage diminishes the memories of the first loss. Why should it? It must be wonderful to find another partner if the relationship brings happiness. The new marriage includes a welcome return to the familiarity of a coupled community. Those of us who do not expect to marry again—very few expressed hopes that this would happen, some expressed no inclination—must continue to develop new communities for ourselves based on independence, old and new friends, new-found interests and, often, abilities and strengths of which we were formerly unaware.

〜 〜 〜 〜

Susan's Story (Second year)
Susan, like Pat, was in the second year when she responded. Her husband, William, had cancer in 1978. It was cured by radiation. A recurrence in 1982 was cured by surgery, but in 1989, an inoperable tumor developed between the back of his throat and his skull. "William developed severe head pain and soon found it difficult to swallow or speak. He grew steadily worse and then collapsed at home. After seventeen days in the ICU (Intensive Care Unit) and on a respirator, I had to make the decision to let him die." William was 64.

Susan and William had been married "38 2/3 years" when he died. They had three children, one of whom lived close to them. There was one grandchild. Susan is an Episcopal priest. I assume she began her studies for ordination in mid-life.

In response to the questions about memorial services and spiritual support, Susan tells us, "I am an Episcopal priest, so his funeral, which I planned, was of utmost importance to me, and of infinite comfort. My faith, my priesthood and the ministry they entail are my spiritual resources. Throughout these two years, I have been sustained by faith, family and friends." Any expressions of concern were immensely helpful. Vivid in her memory of the early grief process, she writes, "was the sense that his illness and death were all a bad dream from which I desperately wanted to awaken but knew I could not. Regretting all the things I never got to say to him was part of it. Because I had suffered losses previously, I don't think anything I experienced was unexpected except the severity of degree. My younger daughters supported me by their physical presence, their thoughtfulness and practical helpfulness. My older daughter had to grieve away from the three of us."

Appreciation for family support is a common thread throughout the responses: admiration for sons and daughters who came, who stayed, helped, and who continue to be available; gratitude for their loving concern. Extended family members are often mentioned in the same manner. All this, in the best possible worlds, should be a given. We questioned family relationships because conversations and discussions with other women showed us that problems—disappointments—do arise among family members despite the best intentions. Everyone is vulnerable. We all make mistakes. We misjudge, we misunderstand, we overcompensate. We're wounded, all of us, and we're experiencing new situations, most of them very difficult, all of them unwanted. Everyone is off balance. Were there moments when you wished someone would help? Or go away? Were you disappointed? Were you hurt? Were you angry? Could you have done more? Were you unaware of someone else's problems?

When I look back on those first days and weeks, I remember thinking I would be able to anticipate, to some degree, what the emptiness would be for Elizabeth and Jim because my mother died when I was only twenty-four, younger than both our children. I remember speaking with them about the awful absence of their father. I am sure they felt it, although, obviously, not the way I did. They were not living at home. Elizabeth and Rob had been married for five months; Jim married four weeks after Jerry died. The void may not have seemed as vast to them. Although I made several attempts, we did not speak much about their grief; they did not seem to have a need. "Are you all right?" I would ask. "Yes," they would reply. They did not speak often of their father. That was their way. On a scale of one to ten, it was a very small disappointment to me. With the passage of time, our daughter and I talk about him often, particularly when something in the political or social arena occurs, and we are sure we know what his reaction would be.

~ ~ ~ ~

Women in the first year group of the project extolled the support of adult sons and daughters, and of their own siblings. "Overwhelming" they said. While the family's immediate presence was vital, these women spoke at length about the importance of continuing concern through phone calls, visits, advice and understanding. Three women wrote specifically about the grief of their children and its effect on themselves: "Our four children, grown, of course, have been very helpful in calling. They all live far away. My daughter has had the toughest time, and I feel needs my help, not vice versa." "I was particularly grateful to my children, sons-in-law and grandchildren for their constant and continued presence, whether in person or by phone or message, and for their understanding urging of me not to fight my tears. Indeed, I could not do so. Their own grief seemed always secondary to their concern for me. Would that I had been as able to support them as they were to support me." "Our three children took the loss of their dad very hard, so they needed help from me: reassurance, consolation, reconciliation. Their distress took a toll of me."

Women who were able to look back on those early days from the vantage of six to ten years or later, seemed to reassess what happened and to offer their thoughts—and their warnings—about how things can go awry. "I think my family has never been particularly good about allowing emotions to surface. They expected me somehow to just keep going, perhaps part of that was their own sense of not knowing what to do. In a number of ways, I became an outcast, someone outside the traditional family they knew. They had a tendency, thinking they were being helpful, to criticize every decision I made, every action I took, which made me feel not only lonely, but insecure." "I don't know if we were very supportive of each other. I was bad, so stricken myself, and so were they. My children all had bad problems, it seemed. Our balance was upset by his death, and we were all reeling with our own anguish."

Other women, writing about siblings and parents, also tell difficult stories: "My mother was unable to share feeling and doesn't 'do grief' so that was hard." "My sisters and their husbands tried to be helpful but really did not know how, and their attempts to take one or two of my children for short visits did not work out well." A woman looking back more than ten years gives us this scenario, "In a huge family, members give according to their own available gifts. Especially appreciated was the support of my critical decisions even when my judgment was flawed. Later, help was similarly offered for the process of unraveling mistakes. Less supportive have been well-intentioned, grieving grandparents who lived nearby and tried to help bring up the children. Giving too many material things and too much money too early to young children is detrimental. To build up a very young grandson as the 'man of the family' with the expectation that he will then fulfill the dreams of his father, who died too soon, is too heavy a trip to lay on a youngster. Even when it is done with love, and through the very real grief of a grandmother."

In all, thirteen women wrote of their sadness at family actions and reactions. Their reports are greatly outnumbered by positive stories, one of which I want to add to our discussion because it raises an important point. This woman, whose husband died six to ten years ago when he was only 55, writes, "I have three sons and a daughter. They were most supportive in being on hand and encouraging without smothering me with advice or thinking they had to look after me." This brings up the concept of taking care of Mom. If you are in your 60s when your husband dies, I'm willing to bet that your adult children, in private and, depending on your interpretation, in either selfish or serious moments, do wonder if their father's death immediately places an additional demand on their relationship with you. In some cultures, it certainly does. In ours, where independence is so prized, the idea of Mom having to be taken care of seems ridiculous to everyone. It occurs to me that these concerns may explain some of the absences or lapses we see in our children's grieving. Mother and Dad together are a strong team. Mother alone?

On the same subject, from a woman who claims to be from the older generation, "Another aspect of widowhood with which I have struggled is my relationship with my adult children. I don't want to be dependent but I want their support. I don't want to complain but I want their comfort. I don't want to be intrusive but I want to hear about their lives. I like to visit them but I enjoy the comforts of a hotel although they ask, 'Why can't you stay with us?'"

Writing from her experience during the second year, a responder shares the following, "The greatest help in our mutual grief has been the understanding of his children which has brought a new closeness to our relationship. His children and I have been mutually supportive, as well as his brother and a cousin. My children, brought up in a stoic but loving tradition (as I see it), have been there when I needed them. It has been a quiet support, not demonstrative. His reserved children have gradually come to me." She and another women reporting from a second marriage give us the good news that difficult relations with stepchildren can improve over time.

᷍ ᷍ ᷍ ᷍

Jean's Story (Three to five years)

Jean wrote four years after her husband died. He was 56, they had been married thirty-two years, had two sons, were new to their community. She has remained in their home. During their marriage, as Jean says, she worked "at a variety of things, part-time." She still does. Here are her responses to the questions about his death, her grief and mourning, the funeral service.

"Bill died of a heart attack while we were on vacation. Actually, he died in the hospital where the medical people flew him for emergency treatment. The heart attack was totally unexpected. He had never had heart trouble or illness related to heart disease. It was a complete shock and even now, after four years, it's difficult for me to believe at times.

"The only thing of comfort at his funeral was the familiarity of the service itself, just following the routine of what I was supposed to do. The real comfort was having so many people come from great distances to attend, and having my husband's best friends carry his coffin. As far as the time afterward, it's all a real blur. The grief has never really left me. I have felt like a different person since the day Bill died. Grief can be 'put away' for periods of time, some longer and some shorter, but I don't really distinguish separate parts of grief. It's just always there. I remember that in the beginning the best support was from people helping me to keep up a social life by inviting me to lunch and dinner, or to spend a weekend. I was sustained by my religious belief that somewhere, sometime we will be together again.

"I have never been able to talk to anyone in my family about my grief. It's too painful for me, and my sons have been reluctant to share their feelings. They are, however, very supportive in every other way. They spend lots of time with me and I know that they care very much about me."

≈ ≈ ≈ ≈

In direct response to our question about the grief process being "as expected," two women found it so. A third, a nurse, wrote that she understood the grief process and added, "but I think what unnerved me most was being able to read without comprehending what I had read." Several others had the same reaction, an unexpected result of their situations. Personally, although I read a great deal, I remembered little—and that only vaguely. There were a lot of mysteries at night. I do remember going through Rosamund Pilcher's *The Shell Seekers*, one of the year's best in 1989. My mentor friend gave me her copy of C.S. Lewis' *A Grief Observed*. I felt obliged to read this wonderful book. I have returned to it more than once.

Women wrote about unexpected occurrences: disorientation, fatigue, loss of self-confidence, feelings of abandonment, shock, and bone-deep sadness. One woman considered suicide, asking, "Why didn't someone warn me?" Sudden floods of tears are part of almost every story in the project, but a few women wrote that they could not weep, one saying that she had not cried at all, much to her surprise and dismay. Women told about their anger: "He didn't take care of himself." "We had no time to talk to each other about death." "We didn't discuss about finances." When read in context with the other responses, this anger seems to be more like a black hole of sadness.

Some of the women whose husbands died following lengthy illnesses reported that they had done a lot of grieving during the months or years before the end came. "His ordeal was over, my grief as well," one woman said. Another, like Caroline, wrote of the deep sadness she experienced during his time in a nursing home. Although I thought my own grief began with Jerry's death, I can see now I was already grieving over his illness and its potential. During the three years we battled cancer, we concentrated on cure. I realized that cancer is a death threat but I really believed we could win our fight. Until the last six months, he was doing quite well although we both knew chemotherapy would no longer be helpful. Then, when blood counts changed alarmingly, there was hospitalization, two weeks at home followed by another hospital experience and, finally, with help from hospice, home-time until his death. During the last two weeks, I could not speak the possibility that he was dying. Someone said I was in denial. That made me angry.

While Jerry was alive and in some control of his situation, I could not admit the possibility of death within a few days. The idea that you might speak something into existence occurred. One dear friend, a hospice advisor, told me to expect his death in the next week. "He'll be here longer than that," I said to myself. And he was. That was important to me. Another friend called to say she had heard he was dying and asked if she could do something for us. She, herself, was suffering from cancer and would die a few months later. Grateful for her call, I told her there was nothing she could do at the moment and that I did not believe his death was imminent. I could not agree that he was dying. I couldn't say it even though I knew it. I would not accept the psychobabble of "denial." Certainly I was grieving. I believe Jerry and I were grieving together. Because there was still life, there was still hope. Was that grief different from my grief that followed? I know now that much of my experience following his death was the result of the double stress of the three years with cancer and the life change that occurred when he died. How deep that distress was did not come clear until I was able to review those months from a distance of several years, and from the written results of this project.

Are there any constants, any specifics in the work of grieving? Stages of grief have been acceptable for years. While I believe the descriptions of these grievings, I do not believe we experience them in a specific pattern, or that each of us experiences all of them. We handle what we need to with differing actions, timing and results. We do what we have to do. There are so many decisions to be made, so many responses to demands during these most difficult of times when other people do not understand what is happening to us any more than we do, ourselves.

≈ ≈ ≈ ≈

Katherine's Story (Three to five years)

Katherine and Ed had been married twenty-three years when he died at the age of 59. They had moved into a new home where she still lived when she responded to the questionnaire. They had no children. Katherine was an editor. She retired two years before she joined this project but still does "a little free lance and some general volunteer work." Here is her story.

"Ed had been disabled by emphysema for six or seven years yet his death was unexpected by us. He was not hospitalized until the last day. That afternoon, still fully alert, he declined further treatment, aware that he would die within a few hours without a respirator. We returned home. He died quietly around midnight. I was with him and so was his cat, as he had wished." It is Katherine whom we quoted earlier as saying, "Of course, his death wasn't really unexpected, its imminence was just denied."

Katherine continued her story, "There was a simple, rather hasty memorial service here in our church. It seemed important to me to have it, but it was not particularly meaningful to me. Since Ed was British, the actual funeral and burial were in England. I found the tradition and ritual had a rightness to it that was very comforting. Of course, four weeks had passed so I was in a different state." About her reactions following his death, Katherine said, "I was surprised by the sheer length of my grief and by the fact that the pain did not diminish gradually. I felt as stricken after eighteen months as I had after one month. I was still crying constantly when alone, and I felt guilty about being self-indulgent. Then suddenly, after two years, the clouds lifted and I felt normal. Now I hear from professionals that, contrary to the popular view of one bad year for a widow, two years is just as likely. Or more."

The support she received Katherine described as "the usual—family and friends—and a counselor, but my job was probably the most steadying factor. Immediately after Ed's death, I poured my heart out to a minister I scarcely knew. He was kind and helpful, but I did not continue my relationship with him or his church. As far as family members, they helped enormously by just being there and by my knowing I could count on them. I'm sure having children would have been an enormous help in that period. (I think of my mother's widowhood.) Two of my brother's children have moved within two hours of me, and they are a great joy and support. Since Ed's family lives abroad, there was less contact, but we have become closer since his death."

The population of this project includes several younger women with small children. Obviously difficulties were enormous. In response to the question of help and support she welcomed, one of these women said, "All kinds, from more food than we could eat, to donations, to invitations to all of us, to telephone calls and letters. It was overwhelming. I needed to be alone with our children a great deal and so declined a lot of offers. By the time I needed them more, six month later, the offers had tailed off naturally as people did not know I needed them. I had three friends and two sisters who were always there for me and without whom I would not have survived."

Another response, "Several things have helped me through the twenty months at this point: family, friends, an extremely sensitive and astute psychiatrist, and a note from a college housemate with whom I had had no contact since the 1950s. In her note she spoke of her own past experience of the sudden loss of her husband, and of her lesson. She had thought she had to be strong for her young children and found, in the long run, that was a mistake. She urged me to learn from her mistake and seek support and help from any of the many sources which are available these days."

Another response, "My mother, who was a widow, came right away and stayed for about a week and was very helpful, especially in practical ways. I realized that my experience with grief was very different from those described in the books that were just beginning to come out in the late sixties. I did not feel angry with God. I was truly sorry for my children that their father would not be there for them in their teen years, and for myself that our plans for the future would never happen. But I felt a sense of joy for my husband that he was with God. It was helpful later to talk with other widows who had a strong faith themselves and whose husbands did, too, and who had similar experiences as mine."

The benefit of talking to and sharing with other widows is a common thread running through the responses. In some cases, the supportive widow has long been a good friend. In others, she is a new friend encountered during travels or social events. The possibility of finding joy in new friendships is part of the healing process. Being open to it is important. The added joy in finding, again, friends you have not seen in years cannot be over estimated. It is astonishing how often these friendships reappear. Reunions, returns to previous home areas, "I-just-heard-about-it" letters, travel, the small world syndrome—these all are opportunities for renewal. More will occur if you make some effort to reach out. This urging for outreach is another common thread running through many of the responses.

≈ ≈ ≈ ≈

Responses to the project's questions about spiritual resources also lend themselves to many thoughts in common. Basically, there seem to be two distinct approaches: those that speak of the need for and benefits of community whether of church, faith or friends, and those that indicate sincere preference for going it alone. There were several responses of "None" that probably indicate a true assessment of an internal and a very personal situation.

Going through the responses to make a count of those who specifically mentioned the words "God," "clergy" or "church," I was interested in the ayes and nays in the various groupings. In the first year, five responses spoke of reliance on these spiritual resources; eight made no or very little mention of them. The second year group shows four to two; three to five years: ten to ten. In the six to ten year group: thirteen to eight. More than ten years: equally divided, three who used these words, three who did not. When I checked back to the earlier question of whether memorial services were helpful, using the same criterion (mention of God, clergy and church), I found that many more women used the terms in positive ways.

I wonder if the word "spiritual" was off-putting. Had we asked each participant for a definition of spiritual resources, I believe we would have received a wondrous assortment of individual thoughts as well as some extremely succinct negatives. We had no intention of keeping "spiritual" specifically in the realm of organized religion. Nor did the women who responded. When asked what spiritual resources she relied on, one said, "To date, my own. Maybe next year I'll have another idea or comment." Other responses: "Spiritual resources? What are they? For me a sense of preordained insight leading me to read various useful texts, preparing me to anticipate his death, encountering friends whose experiences illuminated mine. He and I preferred to go through this bout with cancer as privately as possible, so neither of us turned to conventional sources of spiritual comfort." "Not much. Church was zero help as new pastors were on duty. Two former ones frequently called. My religion did not pull me through." "No particular spiritual resources. While I believe in God, I have not resolved in my own mind whether I believe in an afterlife. This does not bother me." "Can't say as I had any. That isn't my long suit. My only thought along these lines was, 'He's okay. Now it's time to take care of me.'"

Karen's Story (Three to five years following his death)

Karen's husband, Richard, suffered from heart problems. He was 67 when he died; she was several years younger. They had been married for thirty-seven years, had one daughter, five sons and one grandchild. One family member lived near them; five lived at a distance. Karen said that Richard had "partly retired" before he became ill. She did not work during their marriage and says she has not worked since.

"My husband had his first heart attack in 1960, and first coronary bypass in 1971. He had many other physical problems but handled them well and never complained. His last coronary bypass was in November 1985. He was in and out of hospital constantly from then until he died. We had been home only five days after three weeks in ICU where they had tried the newest medicine and finally told us no more could be done, so we flew home in a hospital plane. Richard was in the local hospital for the final twelve hours in an effort to keep him more comfortable. Our children were with us when the doctor said it was time to let him go peacefully."

About the memorial service, Karen said, "The familiar ritual was comforting. A quote from Benjamin Franklin read at the graveside service was especially comforting." Of her grief she says, "the bone-deep loneliness was the hardest to bear, no matter how many people were around. That, and the loss of a sounding board to bounce ideas off, a sympathetic ear, a shoulder to cry on, someone to share a laugh with. Unexpected was the loss of self confidence when I would say, 'I can't possibly do this' or 'I can't possibly go there by myself.' Or I would be sure that 'no one wants an extra woman at a party or on a golfing or a skiing trip.'"

Karen writes that she had lots of support. "Most heartwarming was the large number of friends who attended the two memorial services or communicated in one way or another. My family was the greatest possible help. Our six children, in teams of two, took over all the immediate and painful decisions that had to be made. Our only daughter spent the first two nights in our bed with me. My only sister was always available. She and the children saw to it that I was never left alone until I was ready for it. My son gave me his new puppy so I would have company. Later, they planned trips and went with me. All of my family and most of my in-laws were extremely supportive of me." As far as spiritual resources, Karen said she counted on none.

⁂

Several women spoke of sources of support that were particularly helpful to them but did not involve institutional religion or counselors. The healing powers of art, music, animals and nature are mentioned often, indicating a change from self-reliance to involvement beyond one's own devices. These supports are available within the communities of organized religion, but many looked for and found them elsewhere. Again, the common thread of moving out into the world, into a community of your own choosing and sometimes of your own making.

If there is a trend in the responses to this question of spiritual resources, it is that praise for the help of church communities and faith occurs more often as distance from the date of death increases. "God, special friends from church, at first just to cry with and later to begin to help me begin to talk it through. My faith has always been very personal and I think, particularly since our move to this place, has become more centered. I need not only the ritual as a reminder of the continuity, but also the freedom to wander within it and to feel part of the larger community. It is a way of belonging when the traditional belonging, marriage, is suddenly gone. I still have not really dealt with the why? Because I guess the only real question is why not?" "While I attend church very regularly with my boys, I probably found more help in my own bible study, and explored my personal reactions in faith to this experience, coming out on the other end very whole." "All has come full circle in that I believe my remarriage to a wonderful man was a direct gift from God, and that one of the reasons I was 'planted' here was to bring to bloom a brief recovery ministry in our very large church. I am working very hard on this at the moment." This woman is one of several in the project who speak about recovery ministry and their part in it, which is usually leadership. Another woman tells us, "Spiritual support has come in many forms, from many sources, ranging from the warm spring sun on my back to meditation on a mountain top, from informal support groups to church meetings, from special books to rare friends to authentic clergy— and this continues."

Although many women spoke glowingly of the help they received from their pastors, ministers, rabbis or priests, others said their religious leaders were not very helpful. I take this to mean that help subsided after the memorial or funeral service. This was and still is my experience after many years and several Episcopal priests, none of whom knew my husband, none of whom ever asked his name or how I was handling my grief. The priest and friend long gone from this diocese, who knew me and my husband well, has been steadfast in his concern. Occasionally, he returns to Santa Fe, and we speak of Jerry—how good it is to hear him say that name! I would not hesitate to call this man for help if there was a need. If he outlives me, and he probably will, I want him at my memorial service. If not, I will certainly attend his.

≈ ≈ ≈ ≈

The city of Santa Fe, New Mexico, is a small place in the vast Episcopal Diocese of the Rio Grande, so named for the historically important and continually diminishing river that runs through it. The sparse population of people in our very large state is, as we tend to say, greatly outnumbered by jackrabbits. Our churches are also small. Some have only a rector who must handle parish in-reach and community outreach as well as worship and pastoral care. Many volunteers keep things going, as they do in all churches. There are still several friends, lay people, who knew Jerry and speak about his work in the church and the community. I hold the idea that priests are not well trained in how to deal and work, long time, with grieving parishioners. Would I ever broach the subject of Jerry's accomplishments or my grief to those priests who are new to our church, who did not know him? I think not. The real question is, should they?

Further comment on this subject came from a woman who is in the over ten years group, as I am. She said, "My feeling is that often, although not always, male clergy in the institutional church frequently are too busy for in-depth, ongoing spiritual support. They may also be insecure and threatened by an off beat, strong-minded woman and, therefore, are unable to offer all that might be wished. On the other hand, the expectations may be too high."

For six years, I had the privilege and good fortune to serve as a member of the board of the College of Preachers at the National Cathedral in Washington, D.C. This was a great experience, and an introduction to many wonderful people and ideas. The College's mission involves raising the level of preaching by offering continuing education seminars and conferences to priests, ministers and lay people from Christian and other communities throughout the world. Board members are encouraged to attend conferences whenever possible. I sat in on the opening evening of a conference on grief and grieving given by the Rev. Dr. John Claypool, a well-known and remarkable author, preacher and teacher. Present, also, were more than thirty clergy who came for many reasons, one of which stands out in my mind. A priest related that she had come to her parish a year ago. Within this year, she had performed more than twenty-three funeral or memorial services. She was overwhelmed by her grief. I had not given any thought to the sadness of the church rector or the rabbi who grieves, if one may put it, from the other side. The three women priests in the project must grieve from both sides.

☞ ☞ ☜ ☜

Betsy's Story (Six to ten years following his death.)

"Tom and I were on vacation. Late in the afternoon, he complained of not feeling well, of vague symptoms. He said he wanted to lie down; he did not want to go to the emergency room; he would be all right. I went to dinner. On my return, I found him unconscious. He died instantly of a massive coronary."

Betsy and her husband were in a second marriage. He was 62 when he died. They had been married for seven and a half years; each of them had three children from their first marriages. Two of her children lived near by. During their marriage, Betsy worked as a registered nurse and counselor; Tom was in sales. She has continued to work since his death. Here is what she has to say about the memorial service and her early grieving. "My minister was a Godsend. He made arrangements for the services, did the notices in the papers. I love the liturgy of the memorial service. Later, Tom's sister, her husband and I took Tom's ashes to a lake spot that had great meaning for us all. Our minister helped us plan that part of the service.

"I had written a forty page paper on grief in my graduate program about four months before Tom died, so I had some understanding of the process, which was a comfort, but I didn't know how physical and overwhelming grief is, hurting to the deepest part of one's self. When it comes, it is! C.S. Lewis describes it so well in *A Grief Observed*.

"I welcomed practical help: food, driving family members to the airport, and so on. I appreciated people who would talk about Tom, listen to all the details I needed to tell, over and over. I appreciated people who called and sent notes, and those who could be with me in my pain. The support of my kids was wonderful.

"All through this time I knew underneath that God was with me. Early on, I had a level of acceptance that I wouldn't have had if I hadn't had ten years of sobriety in Alcoholics Anonymous. I could grieve. I could talk in my group. I could not handle the regular church service because the music undid me, so I went to the earlier service where music had no part.

"I believe my having been divorced and having made a new life including supporting myself and managing my finances helped me to adjust. No major changes were necessary in those areas. The most pain came from losing someone who was the love of my life. I was his. We loved each other and rejoiced in each day we had. I did not have to deal with guilt or regrets, which so many people do. One's life will be different, but still rich and fulfilling."

⌒ ⌒ ⌒ ⌒

Judith's Story (Six to ten years following his death)

Judith's husband, Gene, died at the age of 70. They had been married for more than thirty-six years. One of their two adult sons lived near by. At the time of his death, he and Judith were newcomers in their community. Judith moved to a smaller house a few years after Gene's death. Her outside involvement was and is volunteer work. She begins her story this way, "My husband died within twenty-four hours of having become very dizzy, just after I had left on a bus to watch the big holiday parade in our city. A neighbor took him to the hospital. No one could reach me. When I came home around four o'clock, the neighbor told me what had happened. I went directly to the hospital. Gene looked fine and said he would be home tomorrow. At three o'clock the next morning, the doctor called. I went to the hospital but never saw my husband alive. After an autopsy, a large blood clot was found. He had died of a pulmonary thrombosis.

"Although I am a religious person, after consulting with my sons, we decided against any memorial service. I read the service myself the day his ashes were scattered at sea by the Neptune Society. I am not in favor of memorial services and seldom attend any at all. I feel that the service is not for the departed person, and often a eulogy means nothing.

"Both my sons were with me for several days. I guess I was in shock. I would hear a bit of music and dissolve, tears and all, even though music was his love, not mine. Within a month, I decided to move the twin beds out and take over a double bed from the guestroom. With that change, I could face the bedroom alone, my radio going all night. For the first four months, my younger son, who lived just a few miles away, came each weekend to see what progress I was making with settling the estate. We were in trust, so that made things relatively easy. I did spend a great deal of time at the copying machine. I found some neighbors were very kind. After the first flush of interest in my being alone, most people just wandered off. Two good friends continued to take an interest in me. I am a fairly independent person and was glad to be busy playing golf and continuing my volunteer work. That year, I decided to attend my 45th reunion at Smith College. I had never been before. It was a great idea.

"I have become more of a regular churchgoer, now enjoy the music, and have become a hand bell ringer. I like that sort of fellowship."

≈ ≈ ≈ ≈

Beverly's Story (Six to ten years following his death)

Beverly tells about her husband's death at the very young age of 46. Jack was a psychotherapist; so is she. They worked together, had no children, were well established in their community. She writes, "My husband was the picture of health. He didn't smoke, rarely drank, exercised regularly, was slim and muscular, and respected a healthy diet. He was diagnosed with cancer. He died at home six months later, after several hospitalizations. I had just turned 37.

"Our two dogs were very important! They gave me love/ attention/company while asking little back, gave me a reason to keep going—creatures to love and care for.

"No services were held. We discussed this prior to his death and both agreed. People were very judgmental about this. Our memorial service was about six months after his death, when our beloved dogs and I revisited what had been a favorite family recreation spot, and I scattered his ashes in the woods, winds and water.

"About my grief, there were flashbacks to unpleasant scenes and physical deterioration, pain, sweats, chills, tubes, sores and more. I knew from my work as a therapist that this was common but was unprepared for the vividness and persistence of the images. We had worked in the same practice, so I had to deal with everyone else's questions, distresses, etc., with co-workers, patients, family. I had to pick up a number of his patients and help them deal with their grief over losing him!

"Early on, I was most supported by the company of friends, especially one woman who was always available. It was healing just to not have to be alone while doing such simple things as cleaning the house, washing the car. Later, being invited out to eat was a great help. Later, much later, being able to talk over what I had gone through in caring for him helped. As for spiritual resources, I have none except my own personal belief system."

⌒ ⌒ ⌒ ⌒

Stephanie's Story (More than ten years following his death)

"He died suddenly on a bright May morning. The rescue squad didn't come. I ran down the hall to summon a neighbor, a doctor. The details of that morning will never leave me. The first relief from the numbness was telephoning our four children who lived, three of them, on the East Coast, one on the West. Airplanes are marvelous. The children were home by early afternoon." Stephanie and Fred had been married, as she wrote, "a few months more than forty years." He was 72 when he died. They had two sons, two daughters, five grandchildren. None of them lived close by. Stephanie had worked during their marriage once the children were grown. After Fred's death, she became deeply involved in creative writing classes.

"I have never been a religious person. The service was not helpful for me. My husband and I were members of a Temple, but we had not been active although he had been deeply involved when a different rabbi was in charge.

"As a psychiatric social worker, I was aware of the steps of the grief process. I had developed the Grief Treatment Department at Family Service in our city and helped many widows. I was aware of denial, of anger. I knew my own tendency to intellectualize. I knew I couldn't be objective. I sought psychiatric help. The most helpful thing that occurred in the early stages of my grief was the arrival of a friend who appeared at my door a few minutes after I returned from the airport after saying goodbye to the last child. She insisted I go out with her to an art show. Later on, I appreciated talking to other widows about their experiences. But what I found most helpful for me was to write letters to my husband. I wrote a letter every day for about two months, in a beautifully bound book I had saved for some special purpose. In those first weeks, a young rabbi, who knew my husband, was helpful. At my request, he had conducted the funeral service. He also spent a lot of time with our children and me, recounting some of my husband's humorous statements. That was helpful in the first weeks."

⮑ ⮑ ⮑ ⮑

Connie's Story (More than ten years following his death)

Connie and her husband, Robert, had been married forty years when he died, suddenly. He was one month short of retiring from a large corporation. None of their four children and five grandchildren lived near them. Connie writes that she moved two years after Robert died because she needed a challenge. As she journeyed beyond the horror of her husband's death, challenge became her strong suit; love of nature always ran close second. She was a wonderful, fearless volunteer. Here is the first part of her story.

"Robert died around four-thirty in the afternoon on August 6, ten years ago. Our son, his wife and the two of us were playing tennis the day we arrived at our summerhouse. We had driven for five hours, joined our son's family on the dock, started our boat, and raced down the shoreline, waving and shouting to friends on their docks. We returned, climbed up the seventy-five steps to the house, were challenged to play a couple of sets of tennis and in the middle of the second set, he died instantly. I felt that I had killed him!

"I will never forget the agonized scream from my son as he leapt over the net and ran to his father. That scream echoed in my head for a long, long time!

"The island friends pitched in. Food poured into our kitchen as the family members arrived—nine in all. We were all hyper and calmed only slightly when the island minister arrived. We were able to plan the memorial service. My son-in-law would play the recorder. At the service in the cemetery, we used a long, long poem my husband had written. Our women friends created a magnificent rug of pines, forget-me-nots and other flowers for the grave.

"You asked me what was unexpected about the grief process. What was unexpected for me was a phone call from my husband's secretary—poor lady—the day after notifying me that I was no longer covered by my husband's company insurance.

"I really appreciated the mail. I lived for those notes. I answered them all. Often, if someone rang the doorbell, I did not answer. I was unable to accept callers for quite a while. My spiritual resources? None, or perhaps my own"

∽ ∽ ∽ ∽

Writing more about that fateful day, Connie said, "I thought that I had killed him!" Two other women, one whose husband drowned while scuba diving, the other who died when his horse fell on him, wrote similar statements of self-blame. "If only I had been with him." "What if I had been a better rider and could have gotten help more quickly?" A friend whose husband fell to his death as he worked with two day laborers said, "What if I had told those men we couldn't use them that day?" These thoughts occur. They are terrible. They add immeasurably to grief that is already overwhelming. The harsh truth is that your husband made the decision to play tennis, to dive, to ride that horse, to carry those heavy rocks. You were not in charge of him, his decisions, his life—or his death. Does that make it any easier? Not at first. Our lives are filled with "What if . . .?" and "If only . . ." But really, we were not and are not in charge.

≈ ≈ ≈ ≈

Of the many letters returned with the questionnaires, one was particularly provocative, serious and wise. In part the writer said, "In the last ten years, I've thought a lot about widowhood, it's meaning to me, how it's affected my friends. Widowhood is a stage in the continuum of the life cycle. Some lucky women escape it, just as some of us don't reach the last 'golden years.' To me, the stages of widowhood often seem a lot like adolescence: finding an identity, problems with sexuality, the need of peer support."

Another writer sent this letter. "Dear Shirley, How pleased I was to hear from you and receive the questionnaire. I am so pleased, also, to contribute my recent experience, having it so fresh in my mind, to such a valuable project.

"My life with my husband was rich and fulfilling, and it gives me a tremendous sense of satisfaction to be able to have input in an area about women which has been much ignored. As I read your story, it was astonishing that we shared so many of the same roads as we related and coped with the loss of our spouse. The questions, incidentally, became a form of therapy and I discovered much about myself during the writing process. As a result I have come to a few conclusions, for whatever they might be worth.

"The deep grief and anguish appear to be the feeling of not having that special person in your life, coupled with fear.

"Allow yourself to face all of your feelings, as it does help to get through the extreme feelings of grief and on to the road of healing.

"Find someone with whom you feel safe, who allows you to express these feelings.

"Focus on liking yourself. Miraculously, it overflows to others."

As I read this letter, I was struck by her phrase, "coupled with fear." It is apt, accurate and very insightful. Of the many emotions that can be overpowering, fear is one of the strongest. Name the fear, silently or aloud. Use whatever you believe to be the resources available to you. These lead to the safe places we must find. If going home to a dark house is stressful, turn on the lights before you leave. If you are afraid to be alone, get a pet. If you are afraid you cannot go on, do as one woman suggests, "Get up, put one foot in front of the other, get busy. Tell someone your problem. Share." What we cannot do is go through this time alone, permitting grief and fear to fill us so completely that there is no place for hope. If you have deep inner resources, use them. If you profess no religion but believe in the resilience of the human spirit, let it strengthen you. If you have deep faith, rely on it. Does climbing up into the hills bring you peace? Do it. Is a long walk on an ocean beach therapeutic? Go there. Travel. Play bridge. Go out with your friends to lunch, to dinner, or even to breakfast. Take up tennis. Read. Listen. Laugh. Pray. Try deep breathing. Try the discipline of scheduled exercise. Let your mind rest. As the letter says, learn to focus on yourself. This is not selfish; it is vital. With your own work, with whatever you can call on, and with time, the fear does diminish. You find the safe people and the safe places.

4

☙ Health, Counseling, Anger ☙

One way or another, the effects of stress and grieving take their toll on our health. We wanted to learn how women handled—or did not handle—health problems in the early years.

Mine were odd. I broke bones in my feet. This situation could be a field day for a psychiatrist. It was for several orthopedists and physical trainers. It began some months after Jerry's death. Our daughter, her husband and I had traveled to England and Italy. Returning to Albuquerque, New Mexico, we followed the signs to baggage claim and took our places beside the proper carousel. I admit I was practicing my independence when I reached for my bag. Pushed aside by a stronger luggage seeker, I fell and broke my foot. Fatigue? Carelessness? Balance problems? Just an accident? Or was I really practicing being alone? Who knows? It happened. And it healed. Lots of walking followed, as soon as I was able. Two serious walking trips, one in Ireland with Smith College Travel, the other in the Isles of Scilly off the English Coast. I went with a friend—actually, with Connie—on the first trip. I traveled alone on the second, perhaps to prove that I could. Both were wonderful experiences.

Then, on the second and very difficult New Year's Day after Jerry died, I attended a party, alone and reluctantly. I tripped on a loose carpet and fell again, breaking the other ankle and heel, cutting my face with the glass I held in my hand. A few stitches, and a serious joint injury that will never mend completely. I still walk, helped by acupuncture, Pilates, physical training, and sensible shoes—how I miss those now-forbidden high heels. Although I doubt these fractures were the result of anything other than accident or negligence, they occurred and I report them accordingly, along with incidental fractures of three toes.

When I was in our local emergency room for an X-ray on one of those toes, the young technician apologized to me for taking such a long time. He said he was having a difficult day, his first back at work since his father's death the previous week. He told me he still lived at home and was very close to his dad. I asked about his mother. "She's doing pretty well," he said. He had to take a second set of pictures, so we had more time together. I was purposeful when I told him how sorry I was for his mother because his father's death, for her, meant the loss of her husband and their marriage. "I never thought of it like that," he responded, "that part about the marriage going, too." Being mother, father, son, daughter, brother, sister—this is forever. Being husband or wife, or married, isn't.

Sometimes family members think about each other only within their immediate and constant relationships. To think of mother or father as wife or husband, to give them identity and relationship beyond the familial is not always easy, particularly for younger family members. I wondered later if my young friend remembered to speak with his mother about this new idea. Would he discuss it with his siblings, so they could begin to understand what had happened to her and how totally it had changed her life? I hope so. It follows that one might question parents of adult children to ask if they are always able to see and understand these young people who, themselves, have become husbands or wives as well as fathers or mothers.

⪾ ⪾ ⪾ ⪾

Today, I like to think any health problems I might have result from accumulation of all my experiences during what is, to my astonishment, a long, long life. Happily, there have been no more falls. My tolerance for alcohol is reduced to a glass or two of red wine. In the stress department, I am learning to say "no" to volunteer requests without much guilt. Finding things I love to do is becoming more difficult. I eat well. I don't like to take medicine. I have a good group of professional people in both western and alternative medical practices. I workout with a professional trainer. I have lots of friends, some very good ones. I try to walk regularly, but am often tempted to walk another time. I wish I could sleep better. All in all, I think I am in good spirits and good health.

Walking, exercise, sports: all are mentioned many times by the women in the project either as continuing patterns established before his death or as new routines that are particularly helpful. "I hiked every spare minute. My health improved from this." "I finished a house we were building. The builders, who are my children's ages, became my main friends." "I began exercising regularly for the first time about six weeks afterward, and still am, five years later." "I had lost weight during my 'nursing time' with my husband, and have never gained it back. I am in excellent shape." "My mental outlets of doing things I loved in my volunteer career, with significant challenges, travel, ground breaking work and so on, probably kept me as healthy as anything." This woman's strength and determination are obvious. She, like so many others, knows that keeping busy is a good solution. In her statement, she separates physical and mental health. So does another woman, "I think I am now mentally ill—depressed. My physical health has really been okay. Well, perhaps not: high blood pressure, fatigue. My fault, I feel." Two women in the project said that rest was their salvation. From a woman with a positive attitude but a serious concern, "Fortunately, I have remained very healthy: only a few colds, two weeks of back trouble and a few bouts with the flu. I continue to exercise as much as possible because it makes me feel better. There is always a nagging fear of being alone and getting sick—or of falling. I keep shoving these thoughts away." Her concern about becoming ill or injured with no one available to offer immediate help is serious. It is also shared by others. A neighbor of mine and her friend, who are each alone, share this same concern with a third friend whose husband died two years ago. He was ill and incapacitated for a long time, but he was "there." Very soon after he died, the three women set up a schedule of daily morning calls, "to make sure we all made it through the night." My friend wears an emergency response beeper she can activate if she falls and is unable to reach her phone. "Worth more than its weight in gold," she says. "Makes my children happy, too. I wear it all the time except when I'm in the bathtub. Then it's within easy reach." These devices are available to any one— of any age—who lives alone. Why don't we each have our own?

⌐ ⌐ ⌐ ⌐

Anne, whose story we will follow from now on, writes from a perspective of three to five years, telling us, "There is an old concept that widows have a serious illness in the first six months after their husband's death. One piece of advice given me by a physician was, 'Eat right, get enough sleep, and keep walking!' I still follow this regimen, and I have not had any serious illness. My weight is stable and I feel well. Weather permitting, I take a daily walk." Anne's story begins with her husband's death after two days in the hospital. "For twelve years," she writes, "he had had a genetic disease that his doctor told me would eventually kill him. So his death was not unexpected at that time. The family all came, plus family members of my generation, and we had a private, meaningful service at home. This is what he would have wanted." Anne's husband was 68 when he died; she was 66. She joined the project three years after his death.

"My vulnerability was a surprise to me," she wrote, "and still is very real. We were a close couple, and the loneliness still bothers me at times. Yet I live alone, at the end of a dead end street with no houses in sight. It was hard for me because we did not have a lot of friends in this town, and I've had to start from scratch. His death has cut me off from all things to do with hospitals and medical affairs— an involvement we shared—and I still miss that acutely. I really feel fortunate in that I had a happy marriage of considerable duration, and that my husband was not a bed patient until those last two days. My children have been marvelously supportive, and I am gradually making a place for myself in this community. I don't like to intrude myself on people, especially women who have husbands, so when people ask me to do things with them, I am very grateful, still."

Several women, including a few of those whose stories we have been following closely, did not respond to the questions about health. I hope that means they had no problems. In all, twenty-nine of the sixty-seven who did respond said they experienced no changes, at least no major changes. Most of these women were and remained in good health. The positive side of the responses is that so many were able to avoid serious difficulties. Another positive: those who were able to move beyond early problems, regaining good or, in some cases, benefiting from even better health.

Women reporting changes wrote of depression, stress or despair, of weight gain or loss, too much comfort food or loss of appetite. Some had difficulty sleeping. Fright, hair loss, pneumonia, ulcers and high blood pressure—all these were mentioned. Several women suspected that most of their problems began with stress or with carelessness because their attention wandered, they neglected themselves out of habit or because the pressures of their situations were too extreme. Some women developed illnesses whose causes could not be determined.

Helen's Story (First year, continued)

"Having once had a healthy appetite, my lack of desire to eat or cook when alone resulted in much weight loss. The understanding that the center of pleasure in the brain becomes depressed during grief and accounts for this behavior was helpful. Dizziness set in. A few crackers from time to time helped the blood sugar level. I became a chain smoker to break up the tension and tediousness of what I had to manage. Cigarettes became companions to loneliness. Fatigue and stress began to overtake me, from concern over how much had to be done—and fear of the unknown. Having been overweight to begin with somehow made me happy to see the pounds being shed. Three small meals a day could have helped my diet. Some discipline in avoiding smoking certainly would have helped, but I doubt that I had that kind of discipline. Being more gentle with myself and not pressing forward so much in the beginning may have cut down on stress, but then grief would take over. It seemed to be a double-edged sword."

Jane's Story (First year, continued)

"Sleeplessness, early waking! We shared a double bed for forty-nine years, so my sleep habits were changed now that I slept alone. I have taken sleeping pills only on rare occasions, although I have some in the house. I couldn't trust my memory for anything important. I have to keep multiple notes. I didn't dare put anything away, lest I never located it again. Is there any help for absent-mindedness? I function on one cylinder part of the time."

Caroline did not respond to the questions about health.

Pat's Story (Second year, continued)

"Serious weight loss the first year, serious weight watching the second. I take good care of myself, healthy eating habits and regular exercise, because I don't want to be alone and sick. I have had a continuing struggle with depression but seem to be coming out of each setback a little stronger and more confident. I waited too long before I sought bereavement counseling—nearly a year. Peter did not discuss his illness with me and refused counseling, although I did consult our rector. After Peter's death, I tried a hospice group, but all we had in common was widowhood. I am still in therapy for depression but feel I'm making strides there."

⇝ ⇝ ⇜ ⇜

Hospice, the marvelous system that is helpful beyond belief to so many, does not receive high marks in Pat's account. I am sorry to say that our own hospice experience left me with a divided opinion. I did attend one grief session. Unfortunately it was held in our church, in the room where Jerry had taught Sunday school for several years—not a good spot for me at the time. When my turn came, I took a difficult, but eventually for me beneficial, few minutes to share what had happened. I got through my story with tears and was strengthened by the telling. Listening to some stories being told for, as the tellers said, the third or fourth time, with no progress indicated, disturbed me. I did not return for another session because I believed that experience was all I needed or wanted. Months later, I was asked to meet with hospice volunteers to share my evaluation of their work with us in our home. Hospice Santa Fe was in its early stages. In response to their inquiry, I suggested that they remind their volunteers that the spouse, who is attempting to maintain some semblance of order and continuity in the afflicted household, also needs consideration. I understand that this is part of hospice training today.

In our case, when Jerry left the hospital and before he died two weeks later, some of the hospice volunteers who came to us were very helpful. Some were not. The first man seemed unable to settle into our routine. I had not been given any rules about the proper relationship between volunteer and family. I asked him to eat with us and soon became his caretaker. The second volunteer, a wonderful man who is still a friend, was as concerned about me as he was about Jerry. The office called me about the third volunteer, explaining that she was fine, but some people were concerned about how she looked. Out she came for the daytime shift—and she was great. Kind to Jerry, gentle, efficient and loving. He thought she was wonderful. So did I. Her dyed black hair, overly made-up face and bright gypsy clothes were a delightful change from drab hospital attire. Another volunteer sat several nights with Jerry. She was a single woman whose father brought her to work She had been close enough to the dying to be able to tell me what might happen and to help me handle it when it did. After four days I decided I would manage without hospice volunteers. I wanted to sleep in our bed with him. I could hear him and help him if he needed me. He was not eating, but he could still walk. We would be fine together. The wonderful hospice nurse continued to come every day to monitor him. She said she was impressed with the strength of our household. I can never thank her enough for her interest, her loving care and her presence immediately following Jerry's death.

Susan, whom we heard from earlier, reported that she did not encounter any health problems "related to being widowed." Jean said, "My health is good and has not appreciably changed."

Katherine's Story (Three to five years, continued)

"On the anniversary of my husband's death, I came down with a fairly serious illness of unknown origin though very real.

Recovery took the better part of a year and this may have contributed to the length of the intense period of my grieving."

⤳ ⤳ ⤲ ⤲

Judith's Story (Six to ten years, continued)
"I had put on too much weight, so I worked at losing twenty pounds several years after Gene's death. I ate too many snacks with my evening cocktails. The diet took care of that, plus walking many miles each day."

⤳ ⤳ ⤲ ⤲

Karen and Betsy had no serious illnesses. Beverly said she had no health problems. Karen did report that she gained weight, "Being a typical overeater, I turn to food for comfort." She has lots of company.

⤳ ⤳ ⤲ ⤲

Stephanie's Story (More than ten years, continued)
"Except for an increase in blood pressure, I am fortunate to be able to maintain my health. Unfortunately, I tend to deny aches and pains, have to be really uncomfortable to go to a doctor. I still miss my husband pushing me to make the initial move. I suppose if I had been more vocal about discomforts, I might have received sympathy which I thought was missing. I am much more likely to suffer in silence. My understanding of this characteristic doesn't change my attitude."

⤳ ⤳ ⤲ ⤲

Connie's Story (More than ten years, continued)
"I didn't experience any changes. I am a fanatic tennis player and that has, I think, kept me in physical shape. I stress the word physical. Mental? Oh, dear!"

⤳ ⤳ ⤲ ⤲

From another woman, "For the first two months, I did not care if I lived. Then I realized I was a healthy mother and grandmother, and I wanted to spend time with the children. So I kept the usual routine doctor appointments and tried to take care of myself. I finally accepted widowhood, even though I didn't like it." Perhaps here and in other responses to the question of health, there is a continuation of the procrastination of self-care we developed when our children were young. As one woman wrote, "My body is the piece that received the least attention for a number of years, and I guess this form of abuse was not so benign."

There were other responses about health: "I should have obtained help much earlier than I did." "I have an on-going weight problem, not serious, but I always need to lose ten pounds. I go up and down like a yo-yo! A prescription for sleeping pills to help a mild case of depression should never have been renewed time after time." "I am generally in good health and have tried to eat properly and not drink too much—which was a problem for a while." "The first year I lost eighteen pounds, experienced poor eyesight, slightly diminished hearing, and a tear rash—also fatigue. Certainly attributed to grief and its stress." "Had walking pneumonia. Loss of appetite. I would have loved to drink myself into a coma, but impossible in body and thought. Considered suicide vaguely."

Some of the responses were presented with humor, but they had their serious side. "Perhaps more flossing? I hate staring at my face in the mirror!" "No changes of any significance, but I hated having the flu alone. No chicken soup-bringer." "For your entertainment: my husband usually had a dish of ice cream every evening. I started having a dish of chocolate ice cream every night in bed and learned, from pain, that I had gallstones. Am handling the problem by, among other things, switching to yogurt as the indulgent comfort food."

After Jerry died, I did not take into account my existing fatigue. The burdens increased, and I made them heavier by looking for additional ways to be busy. We had spent several years working out at a health club before his cancer became evident, so I did have a strong body. I'm blessed with fairly strong nerves. I had a new house to finish, a dog to care for, friends and family to help me. I should have walked more. I should have rested more. And I should have indulged in simple pleasures, but we had forgotten what these were when Jerry's illness became severe and we turned all our energies toward survival. I needed a relearning experience. Mistakenly, I put this off, partly because of a misguided Protestant work ethic that I thought would rescue me. Our daughter's highly contagious sense of humor was the blessed comic relief that accompanies tragedy and helps to make life bearable. She reminds me that I did and said "some pretty odd things." I was forgetful. I was difficult. I could not make up my mind. Her memories about these are not the same as mine, but when I look back at my notes, hers are correct. Occasionally, she says, she asked if counseling would have been helpful. A good question. We incorporated it into the questionnaire.

The project's questions about counseling are as follows. If your husband suffered a terminal illness, did you and he seek counseling during the illness? If yes, how did the counseling help? If no, in retrospect would you have handled the situation differently? What counseling services did you use or investigate following his death? What benefits came from this?

When Jerry and I first went to Mayo Clinic, we were offered counseling. We did not make any decision about it. In fact, I forgot the offer. I know that my and, I think, his immediate reaction was to ignore the idea. We were both sure that we would conquer the disease. As a woman in the three to five year group said, "To seek counseling, we would have had to admit that he might die." They, and we, had the outsider's view of counseling. We were too private, we would be uncomfortable; counseling was a last resort. So we worked with our doctors; we went to the gym until Jerry's condition weakened; we attended healing services at our church; sought the advice and services of an acupuncturist; followed strict diet regimens; and did not seek help beyond these measures. Why not? We were without any prior experience, we didn't know what counseling could do for us, and perhaps we were afraid to try it. My notes from two years later tell me that I wished both of us had accepted Mayo's offer.

I had assumed that our lack of interest in counseling or therapy was a generational thing. According to the responses, it is not. The pros and cons of counseling came from women of all ages. The final tally shows that more than half of the responders did seek professional counselors. It also shows that women are more open to this kind of assistance than their husbands. (I wonder if women who are dying want to talk about what's happening more than men in the same situation.)

Responses from women in the first year group indicate a varied reaction to the idea of counseling and its benefits: "We sought counseling about a year before his death, mainly for me. But we were not able to find satisfactory help." "Psychotherapy, very helpful!" "Both of us were compulsively private. I still am." "My husband was quiet, New England, bear your own burdens. He never spoke of his death, nor did I press him to do so." Other women said they should have sought counseling or continued with it.

꙰ ꙰ ꙰ ꙰

Helen's Story (First year, continued)

"Hospice counselors came to the house, but somehow we felt imposed upon, and the few times they came the experiences seemed to be flat. Alan did talk to professionals at one point when he had been hospitalized, and found that extremely beneficial. My role was that of feeding information. Because I became his lifeline, that became therapy in itself. He said he often felt the presence and guidance he got from me was more helpful than what he might experience otherwise. Friends allowed me to vent much of what was happening and gave me a tremendous safety net. Many encouraged me, and that seemed to be all I needed."

〜 〜 〜 〜

Jane, in her first year, said they did not consider counseling.

〜 〜 〜 〜

Caroline's Story (First year, continued)
"It never occurred to us to seek counseling but maybe we should have before David lost his mental faculties. It's a new idea to me, and with his health history, might have been helpful."

〜 〜 〜 〜

Earlier Pat wrote about her husband's refusal of counseling, her hospice experience and her problem with depression. Other second year responses show, again, the varied thoughts on the subject typical of every group: "The psychiatrist already knew our family. I was in group therapy with him before the fatal accident. He knew my husband intimately and has been invaluable to me." "My husband did not discuss his illness with me and refused counseling." "We did not seek counseling. I think it would have been beneficial." "No, I didn't seek counseling. I might have, had there been a terminal illness involved." One woman said she consulted her rector, another spoke of friends as counselors.

〜 〜 〜 〜

Susan's Story (Second year, continued)
"Neither of us sought counseling. He died a very brave, stoical, non-self-pitying death. He was not at all the kind of person who shared deep feelings, especially negative ones. I felt closed out of what was happening to him but realized he had the right to die his way, not mine! He went down with all flags flying!"

Jean did not respond to the questions about counseling. We assume none was used.

Ann's Story (Three to five years, continued

Ann's response to a previous question shows her to be, like many, a woman of strength and conviction. She says of counseling, "No, we received no counseling. Nor did I use any afterwards. I think of myself as fairly tough and hardy."

Katherine's Story (Three to five years, continued)

"Although I could not persuade my husband to join me, I saw a social worker for over a year before his death, and one and a half years afterward. It was enormously helpful as general support, dealing with the inevitable guilt and for practical suggestions."

Karen, like Jean, did not answer. Betsy said, "I talked with my minister during the first year. In the second year I sought counseling to deal with some depression—traumatic circumstances following a move." Judith did not seek counseling.

Beverly's Story (Six to ten years, continued)

A practitioner in the counseling field herself, Beverly asked for help. "Talked one time on the phone to a fellow psychotherapist about difficulty coping with my husband's pain and suffering. He basically gave me permission to not have to be 'perfect!' This was very helpful. My husband and I helped each other with everything else. No other counseling before or after."

Stephanie's Story (More than ten years, continued)

"After my husband's death, I had eight sessions with a psychiatrist, a method of treatment I had practiced as a professional, and found it a helpful method in crises."

Connie's Story (More than ten years, continued)

Connie reported that the counseling question was not relevant because her husband's death was sudden. She added, "No, I didn't use any counseling services but eventually, I did question my widow friends, all of whom seemed so cheery. Indeed, I found they, too, had gone through the many stages of shock, etc., etc. I was not unique! Perhaps if any of my family had lived in the area, I would have rallied sooner for their sakes." Connie's response included this addendum, "My husband first saw our second child, a son, when he was four years old. Had I realized, when Steve sailed away from San Francisco, that I would not see him for four years, I would have walked into the Pacific. Perhaps the war years alone with two children, in my early twenties, helped me manage later on. Therapy was not given to our families. Nobody knew about readjustment therapy. We all worked it out ourselves!"

As you can see, opinions vary, so do concepts of what counseling is, can and should do, as well as when it might be used to advantage. Although the question was asked in regard to long-term illness, several women whose husbands had sudden deaths did seek counseling. One reported that she and her young children would soon go into counseling, "Now that they are old enough to understand."

Women in the three to five year group, the most numerous responders, have these thoughts to add: "My husband told a friend that he could not have gotten through the ordeal of dying without me and the church. The same held true for me. Cancer Family Care and hospice were added strengths." "No formal counseling before or after his death, and I would not do it differently. What did help greatly was my previous training and experience as a hospice volunteer, which was invaluable preparation." "I did seek counseling during his illness and I don't know what I would have done without it. Because I am in the profession, I know the value of it; I know how important it can be."

Six of the fifteen women in the six to ten year group reported that they or their husbands, or both of them, worked with counselors: "I had some counseling. My husband, a physician, did not. But he had a lot of support and spiritual direction from a close priest friend." (Some clergy are trained as counselors.) "We sought counseling with separate sources: he with our priest, I with a psychologist. I was aided tremendously in feeling less trapped, less angry, less a victim. I don't know that he helped me deal with the grieving process as much as the dying process. The counseling was invaluable in helping me accept the very difficult time prior to my husband's death." From those who did not use counseling: "Not during his illness. We did not discuss death at that time. I don't believe he wanted to. He believed he would get better." "We became closer but did not seek counseling."

Women reporting from more than ten years: "During his illness, his mother pursued faith healing, sometimes with him. Although I think that was inappropriate for him, it was a real help for her. Therefore, we would not have done differently." "My husband was not aware he had a terminal illness. He discussed his health with his doctor but did not follow the doctor's advice. I wish I had been more sympathetic with him instead of nagging him about taking better care of himself." "No, knew of none available. Now this little town has hospice, and a friend is in charge. Think it would have been great!"

☙ ☙ ☙ ☙

I have two friends whose husbands are in distress, one with a serious heart problem, the other with a brain injury that will not heal. One woman is the primary caregiver; the other visits her husband daily in his nursing home. Neither of them would consider counseling. In my opinion, my friends are not doing anything about their own health—mental or physical. Neither has any idea of what is meant by "take care of yourself." One of them becomes angry, saying she has more important things to do. I have strong feelings about what I would have to call "spousal care." Is there any? I believe that, in some way, the medical world should attend to the physical, emotional and mental condition of the primary caregiver—almost always, the wife. In our case, as the situation worsened, no help was offered, no interest expressed. From what I have observed of my two friends, the situation has not changed.

These women are tired, so tired. They feel guilty if they are not available all day long and into the night to work on the problems of illness, finances and futures. Is this happening to friends of yours? Will speaking to them about it do any good? Probably not. My friend whose husband is at home says there is no time for an afternoon nap, even though she has daytime help. She worries constantly about their finances, and she wonders when she will have the courage to make the decision to place him in a nursing facility. The other friend is, I think, becoming depressed as she watches her husband's mind and body deteriorate, and worries about the high cost of the nursing home and its effect on their financial future. They each consult with doctors about their husbands' conditions. They pay little attention to their own.

During Jerry's illness, it would have been comforting if at least one of his doctors had asked me how I was doing. Perhaps that is against medical ethics. Perhaps that early offering of counseling was all there was. But as Jerry's condition deteriorated, so did mine—physically as well as mentally—because of my extreme fatigue, worry and fearful anticipation.

Without a doubt, severe illness or lingering illness of a spouse has a devastating effect on the non-patient partner. Either one destroys the quality of both lives. Jerry and I were a team. Whenever the doctor saw him, I was there. We were working toward the same goal. Is it time for a new medical specialty that involves an awareness of the needs, and cares for both team members, together and individually?

꠸ ꠸ ꠸ ꠸

We cannot leave the subject of health without looking into anger, an aspect of emotional health. Start with the understanding that emotions are not rational; they are feelings; they don't have to make sense.

The word "anger" comes from Old Norse *angr*, "grief", from "affliction", and from the Latin "to strangle." "Antagonism" is included, plus "rage" and "wrath." I'm not at all sure that, with these definitions, anger is the correct word to describe what we feel. Does our wonderful English language contain the right word? I am more drawn to the definitions and derivations that focus on grief and sorrow, certainly an intense grief, an intense sorrow. My daughter told me I seemed very angry at Jerry's dying, at being alone, at having to do everything myself, at the doctors who failed us—of course they didn't; their expertise did. Now I believe I was suffering from what we might call "widow's days," perhaps "Widow's Daze?" I had to be effective when I was hardly rational. I had to make decisions and respond to demands during, for me, the most difficult time in my life. I couldn't explain what was happening to me and at times, I couldn't handle it. I exploded. Was that anger? I doubt it. I was more saddened and frustrated than angry. Approaching anger from my own perspective, I say that anger needs an existing antagonist. Where is it and who is it? If you can get at it, touch it, then I believe you can be angry. If not, perhaps you're experiencing something else.

꠸ ꠸ ꠸ ꠸

Helen's Story (First year, continued)

"Anger has been minimal. However, one evening I found myself enraged that I was in this situation. I didn't ask to be single or go through this dreaded illness. I had not chosen to be alone, without a husband. At times, I found myself hating the lifestyle, the drudgery of paperwork, unknowns and loneliness imposed on my spirit. I was such a social creature. Yes, the choice was not mine. Also I resented the small slights that occasionally came along."

Helen moves right into the problem we all face: the suddenly singled syndrome. But if there is anger, what or who is the antagonist? I suspect her words and feelings come from deep sorrow because we are where we are and we cannot get away from the situation. There is no cure. Instead, we must go through it, build something better on the other side.

⁌   ⁌   ⁌   ⁌

Jane, who speaks from long life experience says, "No anger experienced nor do I see any reason for anger in my case." Not all women her age react with such gentle acceptance.

⁌   ⁌   ⁌   ⁌

Caroline's Story (First year, continued)

Caroline says she was angry with her husband, "I was angry at David the last two years because he did nothing to help. I was living two lives, dressing, nursing care, driving—everything plus business and financial matters for the family, things that I did not understand completely, and he could not answer my questions. Of course, he could not help his condition, but at times I was angry!" If Caroline had a second chance at this question, might she have used words like frustrated, sorrowful and exhausted instead of angry?

⁌   ⁌   ⁌   ⁌

Pat's Story (Second year, continued)

"I was—and am slowly getting over it—v-e-r-y angry with the indifference of the hospital staff and some of the attending physicians. It has taken me a long time, nearly twenty months, to understand that my anger is really for being widowed and alone."

Pat did have antagonists, but they were indifferent and unreachable. Is resentment a possibility? Because I felt the same way, I often wondered if bitterness was included.

≈ ≈ ≈ ≈

Soon after the birth of our son, my doctor told me I could not be discharged from the hospital because I needed immediate surgery for a very threatening situation that he had been concerned and silent about during my pregnancy. The suspicion was cancer. Nothing was said to dispel this fear. When I told the surgeon and my own doctor that I would go home with our child regardless, they decided we could be at home together for two weeks. Then I would have to return for the operation. Imagine the underlying sadness of those fourteen days of joy! When I came out of the anesthesia, the surgeon told us it was not cancer. Ten days later, he reported that the suspect growth was a sponge left behind during an appendectomy five years earlier. Disbelief, elation and, of course, anger. But at whom? The unknown nurse who had miscounted, certainly not on purpose; the original surgeon who, by custom, had to assume responsibility? The hospital? Where could anger be directed? The end result for me was a spate of internal medical problems that my internist said was caused by resentment. He told me to let it go. So when Jerry died, I recognized the great potential for resentment, along with hurt, sadness, suffering, despair and disappointment—for grief, but not for separate anger, because, rationally, there was not a reachable antagonist. I have come to believe that years of discussion of the grief process and "permission to be angry" have placed anger in too prominent a position. Perhaps only I believe that there are always other emotions included in what we call anger. In discovering and understanding these, might we find that much of our anger simply does not exist? It's okay to feel it; after all, it's an emotion. But don't let it consume you. Look deeper.

≈ ≈ ≈ ≈

Susan's Story (Second year, continued)

"I was angry at William for leaving me to cope with life without him, particularly areas like finances, which I dislike handling. I also resented his absence when first, my son, and later I had to be hospitalized briefly. And turning sixty without him upset me."

≈ ≈ ≈ ≈

Jean wrote, "I was not angry. That was the farthest away emotion. I've known others who were that way and am sure I would have recognized it in myself." Katherine said, "I was angry but not very, and only at myself for not handling the situation very realistically." Ann, "Not angry. Sad, lonely sometimes, cheated out of a retirement in which we could travel together, but very grateful for considerable travel during our life together." Karen, "Perhaps a bit of bitterness at 'why us?' Why not some unhappily married couple? But at the same time, realistically, I had to be grateful for thirty-seven years, fifteen of them on borrowed time, so to speak."

≈ ≈ ≈ ≈

Several women in the project asked, "Why us?" I did, and my husband asked, "Why me?" The very difficult answer is "Why not?" Everyone has to die and, except for suicide, no one can determine how or when. Life is not fair. The reports of anger "at him for dying" and "at God" seem to me to be both futile and sometimes harmful. We can be angry at friends and family, but for how long? It's interesting that no one seems to focus anger on nature, in most cases the real culprit. One woman wrote that she was angry at "fate, or life, I guess." Another, "I was not angry. That is where philosophy enters the picture."

Betsy wrote, "I was angry at Tom for leaving me, and at God for taking him." Judith, "At times I have been angry that Gene died before he had the experience of grandchildren. I have four now, two from each son. These grandchildren are a great pleasure which he missed, and he loved little ones."

Beverly's Story (Six to ten years, continued)

"My only anger was toward the rude, insensitive comments of 'friends' and one doctor. He told me at first meeting, after I requested an oncological consultation regarding my husband's condition, that I would have to quit my job. 'There are always other jobs,' he said. Who did he think would provide us with an income, health insurance, pay the mortgage and all the medical expenses?"

Within the responses there are several more specifics like Beverly's that do provide an antagonist. Connie has already shared her problems with her husband's company. Two others wrote of similar difficulties; neither said whether legal channels were used. Two others: "My anger was directed to the bureaucratic procedures of companies which seemed designed to make life difficult, i.e., transferring title of the car to my name!" "My only anger was encountering, for the first time in my life, the stupidity of male chauvinism, i.e., having to prove to the bank where my husband and I had a joint account for over twenty-five years that I, a mere *ux*, was capable of having my own account."

Stephanie's Story (More than ten years, continued)

"My training made me well aware of my anger, but knowledge didn't erase it. The larger burden of my anger fell on friends whom I did not feel were supportive, and on family members who lived in other cities and who did not offer support I would have appreciated."

⇒ ⇒ ⇐ ⇐

Connie's Story (More than ten years, continued)
"I don't remember being angry with anyone. I wished so much to be able to get control of my constant weeping, so perhaps I was angry with myself."

⇒ ⇒ ⇐ ⇐

Some other statements about anger: "I wasn't angry, only sad for all he had looked forward to and could never enjoy: children, grandchildren, travel, leisure time." "Often my anger is directed at myself, sometimes at him, rarely but occasionally at God. As Shirley did, I finally said to myself, 'Get on with it!' Prayer has been my guide. Now that the pain has turned to ache, I'm not nearly so angry. Reasoning does take root!" "Anger? I focused mine on the tennis ball, the golf ball, the swimming pool water, the hiking trail!" "When I realized I was angry, I also realized I was angry with my husband for leaving me alone, for just disappearing. Once I understood that, I obviously couldn't be angry any longer." "I don't like anger very much. I'm not good at showing it or being the brunt of it. So my focus, when it hits, is, after a good and private cry, to get past it without 'stuffing it,' and to re-focus on what is good, positive, hopeful and beautiful. If you really love and are happy and content with someone and were given 2000 years together, when the 2000th year was up, it still wouldn't be enough. Therefore, it's well to enjoy all that you are blessed with for however long, and to be grateful for the gifts and their memories."

In an earlier chapter, I said that we do not know, or cannot judge, whether unexpected, accidental death is more difficult for the wife than death following terminal illness. Two women, each of them in the six to ten year group, used the question about anger to express these thoughts: "I don't remember anger. That may sound odd. I felt short-changed because the timing was so unexpected, and I was still, I thought, relatively young. But I was not angry. I was—and still am—thankful for the simplicity and peacefulness of an instant death, with no agony of disease and gradual deterioration. I consider us both exceptionally lucky for that" "How could I be angry? My husband's life had been full. The last thing he could have stood would have been failing health or retirement. And anger would have been self-pity. I do not believe that's a positive emotion."

One woman wrote about a different anger, a different focus in a situation not at all unique in cases of terminal illness, "My grief was in the beginning, when I knew what we were facing. Only once did I give in, and it was when I realized there was no hope. He took out his anger on me—which in many ways, made it easier in the end."

⌒ ⌒ ⌒ ⌒

On a very different level, anger, a superficial anger, can occur when we are in a social situation and made to feel vulnerable by a foolish remark. Once a year, three of us meet at a fourth friend's home for talk, shopping, eating, sightseeing and fun. We are all widows. We have a great time together and we enjoy renewing friendships with many of our hostess's friends. Occasionally, when we arrive together at a party, a married friend will say, "Here come the girls!" Women do this more than men. It's thoughtless and, I think, stupid. If we had our wishes, we would have come with our husbands. None of us can do this. I am unhappy when my single status is emphasized by this kind of remark, even if it may be an innocent one. I tell myself, "Smile and forget it." Obviously I can do one, but not the other.

5

∽ Friends ∾
Keeping Old Ones, Finding New

When my friend Kay Halpern and I began reading the responses to the questionnaire, each of us found that we had to limit our time. Occasionally her professional interest as a sociologist and my interest in developing the project had to be set aside. We needed to stop reading, to distance ourselves from the many reminders of the trauma, sorrow and isolation women face when husbands die and marriages end. However, my sessions with Kay often closed on an upbeat because we found so much evidence of strength, courage and the will to move ahead, off dead center, even from those who admitted they had not yet been able to do so. We were impressed by the admiration, good will and appreciation these women attributed to their families, and by their thankful acknowledgement of the great support they received from their friends. The word "overwhelming" used so often to describe their grief and then to value the help of family, now occurs in still a different context. It has become overwhelming gratitude for the caring and assistance of friends and neighbors.

We asked the women in the project to tell us what help offered by friends was most appreciated, how they and their friends dealt with the loss, how changes in relationships occurred. Were barriers raised between them and their friends? Would friends discuss his death or reminisce about good times? What about relationships with other widows? All in all, we said, "Please continue to tell us what happened."

Our statistics, and I am sure most other statistics, show that the majority of parents and their adult children, by choice or circumstance, live apart from each other: a few blocks, a few miles, a few states, occasionally a few countries away. The sons and daughters as well as the parents have their own lives. They have their own communities of friends and neighbors that are quite separate from the community of family. They share the major portion of their time and activities with friends and neighbors. Families that come together after a death eventually separate so the adult children can resume their own lives, in their own mainstreams. Then the mother must look to her friends for her daily support. The phone calls from friends asking how are you, what are you doing, what do you need—the ones that interrupt a particularly lonely time—become a lifeline. "Always there for me" is the accolade our responders use many times in reference primarily to female friends, sometimes to couples although it is entirely possible that the female friends also figure in the couple statistics as do the male friends who are thanked for the practical assistance they provide. Widowed friends are mentioned often. There are also stories of old friends lost, new friends discovered. The status quo has changed. Relationships grow stronger or weaker as people deal with the new present and its future.

In reading the continuing stories of Helen, Jane and Caroline, it is important to remember that they are in their first year. Pat and Susan are in their second. These five women speak to us from immediate experience, from the hardest years. Their stories differ but each is a valid presentation of what happens once the onslaught of widowhood—I think that's a pretty good phrase—begins.

᙮ ᙮ ᙮ ᙮

Helen's Story (First year, continued)

"My female friends shared stories of their losses and allowed me to cry and tell them how I was feeling. Many females, single, widowed, divorced or married, came forth with compassion. It was overwhelming. Male friends invited me to lunch and advised me on financial matters. Many stopped me on campus, some who barely spoke to me before. One married couple strengthened our relationship even more with many visits to their home and occasional outings. One special female friend, who is savvy in business, was a great resource and became a mentor for a while. Our closest friends spoke of the tragic loss, the grueling pain of observing stages of illness, and of missing him. The co-workers at the school frequently remarked Alan's absence and the loss of his valued skills, judgment and caring. Several took time to tell me their fond memories of seeing the two of us together, and of the impression and impact our happiness made on them. Others told me of professional and personal experiences they had with him, making new memories for me.

"I'm sad to say that two very close female friends have cut our ties completely. I called when I did not hear from them, trying to set a stage that would serve as a way we could stay in touch. One of these women often took the side opposite to mine when I spoke of a conflict or when a certain person became an issue. The other would barely recognize what I was going through. Once I was confronted as to why I would continue to wear my rings. That person ridiculed widows who did so. Obviously she is not a widow.

"Being out socially with married friends is minimal. One time the comment from the outer circle was 'widows are a threat to other women because of the husband situation.' I am very open with others who have become or who are widows and am able to listen to their ordeal without judgment. It was so easy to be judgmental before I became widowed. Now I understand why people react the way they do."

⇌ ⇌ ⇌ ⇌

Helen's experiences during those first few months run the gamut from kindness to cruelty. Early widowhood is a hurtful and cruel time. The loss of a close friend is difficult to understand. I believe, however, that the loss of other friends is normal and natural, and easier to comprehend. It might even be helpful. Social friends are busy with their daily work and activities. As new widows, we are occupied with our new concerns; we have to find our way into a new life. In many cases, I suggest that our lost friends or "less friends" are not even aware of what is happening. We are vulnerable. They are busy. We might turn "I wonder what Jane and Bill are doing now, it's been a while since I've seen them" into sadness and even neglect.

Isolation, or a sense of it, can occur very quickly. Several women wrote about the sudden feeling of being left out, of being hurt by what seems to be a purposeful neglect by friends. Sometimes that's not it. Our married expectations of daily companionship, intimacy, conversation, understanding, sharing, enjoyment of being busy together for hours at a time, or not being busy together and considering it time well spent—these are gone. Without him, there's a lot of empty time, time alone, time to be lonely. Our friends can fill only a small part of that terribly empty time. Everyone is thankful for the friends who do help: an hour's visit, a long phone call, dinner and a movie, lunch together, another invitation, a suggestion—these are welcomed, even if not accepted. "Return those invitations" women advise: difficult to do at first, but important.

　　　　◌　◌　◌　◌

Jane's Story (First year, continued)

Many of Jane's friends were already widowed when her husband died. She and John were in their 70s. Helen and her husband were in their 50s. That has to make a difference. Here's what Jane tells us, "This community rallied around me: food, flowers, offers of housing and transportation, invitations to dinner, bridge. I appreciated bear hugs from the men we knew, married ones, too. Everyone needs four hugs a day! Our minister was a great help immediately. All of us were able to speak of my husband easily and naturally. Most of my friends have suffered similar losses so are very sympathetic and supportive. We feel comfortable talking about our husbands but do not dwell on our losses.

"The loss is real; heart-ache ever present. Yet I could not wish him back when his life was not worth living. When I speak to my friends who are widowed, I give them opportunities and leads to talk about their husbands and how they are coping. They are free to pick up on this or avoid it. As far as barriers or friends who are unkind, these experiences have not come to me so far."

⇒ ⇒ ⇐ ⇐

Caroline's Story (First year, continued)

"When my husband was in the nursing home, single women friends and couples were very thoughtful in inviting me out. This has continued following his death but it is not as deliberate. For example, they are including me where I expect to be included. There is not a lot of discussion now about his illness and death. There was more when he was in the nursing home. I've changed the way I talk with my widowed friends. I am much more sensitive, of course. I really want to know how they live alone, how they manage friends, social time and finances.

⇒ ⇒ ⇐ ⇐

Other women shared their first year experiences: "I really cannot separate the support I've had into male, female or married couples. Everyone has his or her own way whether by letter, flowers, food, phone call or visit or even combinations thereof, and every way is special. And I learned to understand the uniqueness of each and to treasure it." "My female friends rallied around with great physical comfort: hugs, hugs, and more hugs. Their support and nurture provided a consistent source of comfort that I could rely on. I found that talking about my husband with these friends, who were such sympathetic listeners, helped assuage the pain. Male friends also were supportive and comforting. However, I also found that I enjoyed being with couples. The intellectual stimulation and conviviality of all these friendships has provided a strong framework for rebuilding my life."

Pat's Story (Second year, continued)

"I have not been an easy widow to support because I put on a façade of well-being and always answered 'Fine' when asked how I was. I'm trying to be more approachable, not an easy role for me. I was helped by friends who understood my need to talk about Peter as a continuing part of my life. And by friends who would say, 'Wouldn't Peter love this?' or 'Do you remember how Peter . . . ?' Some friends wanted details of the illness and death. Others did not. Some are very uncomfortable with my references to him, so we don't see each other as often as we did. I expect I have a newfound sensitivity toward widows, but there are none in my immediate group.

In cases where the death is the first in the community of married couples, people sometimes think they should not speak of the event or the person. They do not know what to say, so they keep silent. Everyone is uncomfortable. Be yourself is the best advice. The bereaved friend has already experienced enough changes. Don't make decisions for her. Say something.

According to some, their married communities develop reactions to them that are often the stuff of novels, often hurtful, most often foolish. As one woman reported, "Initially, several neighborhood wives were very uncomfortable when I was around their husbands. This made me reluctant to ask for male help when I needed it. I resolved that problem by hiring a handyman. Some wives feel that widowhood might be contagious—or so it appears." The idea of a contagious widowhood is ridiculous, of course, but something akin to it does exist.

Obviously, a new widow is not a carrier. She may send a signal that what has happened might happen again. The truth that it will is denied. Fear of death runs deep. It is primitive. Some people cannot or do not want to deal with the reality that now only one half of a known couple exists. Sooner or later, the widow's relationship to her group will change. She—you—will get used to it. It's not as sad as it seems to be right now. You will also find new friends who will gladly accept you as you are.

As Pat wrote, some married women distrust what they think may be the motives of the new widow. I believe the new widow is so absorbed in her own problems that she has no time to turn to someone else's mate. If he makes himself available, that's another problem. Does this happen? Sometimes. Two younger women in the project reported that some husbands did approach them; they "seemed to care too much." Absent the acceptance of an illicit relationship, friendships with these couples are better left to a later day, when, if you want to, you can laugh about the absurdity of the situation.

〜 〜 〜 〜

Susan's Story (Second year, continued)

Susan, like Pat, experienced both warmth and distancing from her friends. "As for support from my friends, everyone expressed willingness to see me, spend time with me, take me out for meals, care what I was thinking and feeling, give me practical advice. One couple, our oldest friends, wanted to talk about my husband with appreciation and humor, especially the wife. This was wonderful. Other old friends seemed to be made uncomfortable by any mention I made of him. I wanted to talk about him. This man lived and is still alive to me, in new ways."

As part of her work, Susan "ran an eight-week grief group the spring after William died, a group in which real bonding took place to the benefit to all, including me." She continues with a surprising account of her experience with some widows, "I feel deep sympathy and compassion for other widows and am very open about my own feelings. I have found women who have been widows for many years to be very unfeeling about my widowhood, much to my surprise. Many of my friends are understanding and supportive, though, and I have so far picked up only the tiniest waves of concern about my single state."

⌒ ⌒ ⌒ ⌒

Jean's Story (Three to five years, continued)

"The best support from anyone was to allow me to talk about what I was feeling and to include me in all the activities in which we were included before Bill died. The person who helped me most was a young man, a friend of my husband's, who came to see me every day for weeks, and was here almost every Sunday for several years. Most of my friends did not want to discuss Bill's death but have always been open to sharing memories. I think I probably avoid discussing his death because I still can't speak of it without tears, and I think that upsets other people, which I don't want to do. It doesn't help.

"If one of the few acquaintances I know who have been widowed asks me, I am happy to give specific examples of what helped me in a very practical sense. This was going back to work! It may sound awful, but I don't relish the idea of spending a lot of time with other widows. As yet, no one in my circle of friends has been widowed. You asked me what was unexpected? Most women are fearful that they will become widows, so they want to avoid thinking about the possibility. They avoided me as an example. Also, I don't think I was excluded socially, ever, because women were fearful of a single, but only because I didn't fit their social pattern of couples."

⌒ ⌒ ⌒ ⌒

Anne's Story (Three to five years, continued)

"We moved here two years before my husband's death. Had been summer people, which is a whole other ball game. He was not well, and unable to carry on much social activity, so we were not out seeking friends. There were few people here who really knew him. One woman, who still has a husband, came to this town, took me out to lunch. She refused to come to my house for lunch, or even after lunch. Something about not wanting to see me in my solo setting, I think. I have not had any good friends widowed since I moved here. In the past, I did not know how to deal with widows but now I would feel free to go see them and try to be of help. After my husband's death, one friend wrote me to say 'You are a survivor!' I took that as a real compliment. I will use that term when writing to newly widowed people."

꩜ ꩜ ꩜ ꩜

Katherine's Story (Three to five years, continued)

"My husband had become withdrawn because of his illness, and our life was difficult. I think people didn't know how to handle his death other than conventionally. I was overwhelmed by the support I received at the time of my illness the following year, and I suspect part of this was an expression of sympathy for his death. I remember that I was distressed that people seemed more concerned about me and my loss than about Ed's. Only one of my close friends is also widowed and, although we live far apart, we have made a much greater effort to see each other and to keep in touch by phone."

Katherine has more to say about her work, "I had a job I loved but, oddly, after Ed's death, when I no longer felt guilty about time spent away from him, I lost interest in the job and never really recovered interest even when good spirits returned. Perhaps I felt that the career belonged to the phase of my life that ended with my husband's death. Of course the situation on the job, unrelated to me, had also changed, so perhaps I shouldn't make too much of this turning away."

⌒ ⌒ ⌒ ⌒

Karen's Story (Three to five years, continued)

"Female friends invited me to go on trips ranging from doing headstone rubbings in England to skiing in Chile and golfing in Bermuda. Male friends included me in golf and tennis games. Married couples who lived nearby always offered to drive me to and from parties, and saw me safely into my house. Others included me in parties my husband and I had formerly attended. I thought, as a single person, I would no longer be included. An older widow advised me to be 'always available' for any invitation—a game of bridge or a trip to Europe. She warned that widows are quickly forgotten if they sit at home, moping. At first, it was very difficult, but, eventually, very rewarding. I always try to include at least two extra women in any dinner party, and more at a large gathering. Only one couple seemed to avoid me. The man had been a beau forty years earlier. I felt it was completely ridiculous but flattering to think I could be a threat. The very last thing on my mind was developing a romantic relationship with any man!"

⌒ ⌒ ⌒ ⌒

Betsy's Story (Six to ten years, continued)

"Friends were supportive, asked me to do things. My minister was a source of comfort, could handle my grief which so many couldn't. This was true of a number of friends at work who had been through their own losses. Some friends would bring up remembrances of him. You soon learn who is comfortable talking about it and who isn't, and I gravitated to those who were. I think, with new widows, being there and listening is the best way I can help. I think people's thoughtlessness—it is a couple's world—continues, still true eight years later. And there is awkwardness. There are so many who don't know what to say or do."

⤳ ⤳ ⤳ ⤳

Judith's Story (Six to ten years, continued)

"As I said earlier, two female friends stood by me. One couple, long-time friends of ours, suggested that I join them on a garden tour of England. I agreed and persuaded a recently widowed mutual friend to come with us. It was a lovely trip. Gene and I had moved so many times that my close friends are in different parts of the country. We keep in touch by phone often, and I have traveled to see them. About social barriers, I don't think I experienced any, but then I am a loner and don't need a great deal of companionship."

Speaking of relationships with friends who have been widowed, Judith says, "I have tried to help others who have been widowed, and hope I have helped them by taking them out for meals and/or concerts. Unfortunately, many were in the dark when it came to finances, so it was hard to help and not be interfering."

⤳ ⤳ ⤳ ⤳

Beverly's Story (Six to ten years, continued)

Beverly praised the friends who, as she remembers, gave practical assistance: helping her get her car to the dealer's, assisting with cleaning, with painting, and with company. She appreciated friends who let her talk about Jack when she wanted to, and did not probe or ask rude questions. "One married couple was great—older people. With a married couple my age, I felt like a fifth wheel the two times we saw each other. They were very insensitive, spoke about what a great year it had been for them, and seemed unaware of what a terrible year it was for me. I had no desire to socialize with them again.

⤳ ⤳ ⤳ ⤳

Stephanie's Story (More than ten years, continued)

"Some female friends, who shared their experiences with me, made me realize I wasn't alone. Some friends disappointed me by not understanding my grief. Couples fell away. I had wished they would allow me to join them and pay my own way. Husbands wouldn't allow it. I was very conflicted when I felt indebted. It's still hard for me—more than ten years later—to ask for transportation in the evening because I don't like night driving. I found that most married women didn't want to talk about widowhood. The idea was too painful. For a long time, I felt a barrier between our married friends and me. Was that barrier real or a projection on my part? I'm not sure"

⁀ ⁀ ⁀ ⁀

Stephanie, who is a psychiatric social worker, gives us an interesting slant on the friendships that change or disappear. From my own experiences and those of many in the project, married friends may remain close, but not in the same way as before. Social relationships change. New friendships with married couples are rare. The need for balance, for an even combination of male and female, is very strong in the couple's world. The widow's new path differs from the path of married couples, particularly where social events are concerned.

Stephanie's need to pay her own way, and the problem it presents—but shouldn't—is by no means unique to her. Another woman wrote that she had to make it very clear that she would join a couple or a group of couples only if she could pay her part. This is an important point. Paying restaurant bills, sharing them, seems to cause a lot of concern. I have learned to pick up the entire check occasionally, if that will even any debt. Tell your favorite couple they must let you pay your share. Be adamant; let them know you are very serious. I dine regularly with a wonderful couple. He figures the check by calculating the tip and dividing the total bill by three. I pay my third. Occasionally I treat them; occasionally they return the favor.

This independence reminds my of my husband who, though usually quick to pick up a check, sometimes would agree to split the total cost. Individual checks? Difficult for the restaurant, embarrassing for the table. If you are in a large party, try to make payment arrangements before you arrive.

The responder who was able "to make it very clear" to her couple friends that she wanted to share the costs of "evenings out," also wrote about clarifying another situation: single women being seated at the same table at receptions and other large gatherings. She has told her hostesses she does not appreciate this isolation. Another woman, from what she calls the "older generation," wrote that she believes men do not like having "extra" women at the table. I want to disagree, primarily because I believe that women are responsible for these conventions and convictions, not men. However, I admit that, as hostess, should the ratio be very uneven, I would seriously reconsider the invitation list unless I knew that the men were secure, interesting and gregarious. Many of them are. Because I live in Santa Fe, largely an open society, second thoughts lead me to wonder if the concern about gender and couples is less a generational issue than a geographic one.

≈ ≈ ≈ ≈

Connie's Story (More than ten years, continued)

"I found that my friends, for a long while, steered away from even mentioning Steve's name because I would begin to weep. Eventually I could refer to him, but even that was hard. All our friends were wonderful, except, of course, no one would talk about him." As she said later, "Of course not! The word was out, no doubt, that I would fall apart if anyone did. I wished so much to be able to control my constant weeping. Weepers are not much fun to have around. I was a bad sport for quite a while." Connie joins a few others who said there should be lessons in widowhood. "Why didn't somebody tell me?" she asked.

It seems that the common thread about how our friends react to us in our new lives has two colors, one white, the other black. The symbolism speaks for itself. Women looking back from the distance of a few years have not forgotten what happened. They have made many new friends; they do not miss the old ones who drifted off. In the early months and years, the losses can be devastating. Later, when you can think about them from another perspective, they may be understood. When we were discussing the subject of friends at the Smith College reunion, I mentioned that I had a bad experience I did not yet understand. During the last two years of Jerry's life, we had lunched every week or so with a couple from our church. Two weeks after Jerry died, she called me to set up another lunch date. I arrived, as did she, but not he. I was upset. Why did he stay away? Why had the pattern been changed when I needed continuity, something unchanged in the midst of so many alterations? President Mary Dunn, moderator at the reunion presentation, suggested I ask them why this happened. I asked him because his wife had moved away from any friendly contact with me. Poor man, he could only explain that she had told him not to come because his presence would upset me. Wrong. In thinking about this, I remembered another luncheon years ago, another couple where the husband had died suddenly. Days after the funeral, we invited his wife to join us at noon in a local restaurant. What to do about seating? Leave the fourth chair in place? No, it would speak too strongly of his absence. Before she arrived, we arranged seating for three at a circular table. I don't know if she thought about the arrangement. I know we wanted to do everything we could to keep her close, to let her know she was invited because she was important to us. We spoke about Phil, we missed him but we treasured her for herself. Was our concern about seating important? We thought so at the time.

Much has been said about the sad occasions when friends seem to abandon us. Is it possible that we rush to make judgment calls about our friends because we are going through difficult times? Do we know how our friends feel about death? They may think, as some women suggest, that it's "catching," that it should not be spoken of, that the widow would be upset if it were mentioned. Avoidance occurs for many reasons. Some people who practice avoidance may do it out of what they believe is kindness. Some of us search long and hard for reasons to explain away the hurt a friend has caused. Perhaps we should have been as outspoken as a few of the women in the project. If friends avoided mentioning him, they say we should have come right out and told them that what we needed, and still need, is to talk about him. Some women said they could begin the conversations. Others admit they could not. Or would not. A few acknowledged they found themselves worrying that how they reacted would upset their friends. They might well have discouraged a friend from speaking because they didn't want him or her to be upset, to be made uncomfortable "doing grief" and speaking about death.

A woman from the six to ten year group emphasizes what we have been discussing, "I found a lot of barriers with several female friends. I think that, in a very real way, it is very threatening to some people—some of my married friends—who are afraid that a similar event would happen to them. It sort of felt as if I had a kind of leprosy in certain situations. I think it really boils down to our culture, that it is not open to the commonality of death, and how important it is that we come to terms with it in our lifetime."

Comments from other women tell what they think is important: "Since I talk of him freely, they also do." "We were able to speak of my husband easily and naturally, to share memories." Memories are very important. Sharing them is vital. Except for those few women who absolutely did not wish any sharing, everyone wrote about how wonderful it was, and still is, to reminisce with friends, to remember his special sayings, to laugh about funny happenings, to say his name, often. This is the best help friends can give. It speaks to mutual loss, mutual support. It provides continuity

From what many said earlier and now repeat, presence—being there—is key. Close friends, family, neighbors, these people come. They continue to surround the widow with love and concern. What about friends who are once or twice removed from the intimate circle? If there is to be a memorial or a funeral service, this is where "being there" begins for them. I have attended a lot of services for husbands of women who are not my very close friends. I will have worked with the wife or the husband in some aspect of community or non-profit service. The women seem grateful for my presence, as I was grateful for theirs. When we meet, we find ourselves speaking of mutual experiences within the context of our, for her, new situation. Obviously, these conversations are unlike any I have with women who are still married. "How are you?" from me to them does not have the same meaning as "How are you?" to a friend who is recently widowed. The connection is different. The first asks about health or is merely an idiomatic expression, a greeting. The other asks how she is coping. She knows that, so do I. This is the empathy we spoke of at the beginning of the project. We have been there, we understand, we share a unique language. Does this shed any light on the reasons why some of our married friends seem to move away from us, or we from them? Why we develop new friends and, if we are fortunate, rekindle old friendships that bring mutual advantage? And why many of our present friends, old and new, are widows?

At the start of the project, we agreed that a widow-to-widow relationship, merely because they are widows, is not likely to develop into a friendship. Why would it, any more than having lived in Boston, or wearing cowboy boots? Friendship takes more than that. Not every widow you meet will become a friend. I was startled when a married friend asked me to lunch with someone "because she was just widowed and you two will have so much in common." There was empathy, but a friendship did not develop.

Two women in the project wrote: "I am very open with others who have become widowed and am able to listen to their ordeal without judgment. It was so easy to be judgmental before I was widowed. Now I can understand why people react the way they do." "I try not to pounce on them with advice. When I was widowed I felt that those already widowed were eagerly welcoming me to the club. I hated that!"

Widows can help each other if an opportunity for shared empathy or sympathy does arise. According to many responders, there have been shifts in the way they now approach women widowed earlier than they. Several of our storytellers said they asked experienced widows how they got through the difficult early years, how they coped.

Stephanie is one of these. "I wish I had been more attentive to those who had been widowed before I was. Where making new friends, it's now easier for me to reach out to those who have been widowed. I'm always interested in learning how other women have responded to widowhood, hoping they can teach me new or better ways of coping."

A woman in the first year says, "Only those who have experienced this loss can relate to others in the same boat. Since I am a recent widow, I realize how much I count on those who faced it before me." Another, "I remember when my first child was born, I developed a new respect and empathy for all women who have had babies. Similarly, I now find myself forging a similar bond with those who have lost their mates. Although losing a loved one is a painful experience, the loss of a spouse is singularly poignant. The profound emptiness that results from the deprivation of shared intimacy—emotional and physical—must unfortunately be experienced in order for one to truly empathize with others. The old cliché 'it takes one to know one' is particularly valid when confronting this grief." A strong response with the same idea, "Widows are brave people. Once in a while a thoughtless remark is made by someone who hasn't 'had it' so I just ignore it because they don't know what they are talking about." This from another woman who spoke of the newfound sensitivity she will use when it is called for, "I don't think I had any idea of what they had gone through. Some of the most encouraging notes I had were from widows and widowers, and now I hope I can express my compassion in a more meaningful way."

This last response not only reflects a new sensitivity but also gives a hint about how to frame the notes of condolence so important to newly widowed women—and men. Don't be afraid to move away from those old-fashioned clichés. Use his name, or hers. Recall a shared memory. I wrote to a friend whose husband died a few weeks after Jerry, reminding her of a great afternoon the four of us spent together at an exhibit of weavings at the Wheelwright Museum of Indian Art in our city. They had honeymooned sixty years ago out on the Navajo reservation, near one of the trading posts involved in the show. Campers and great enthusiasts for the outdoors, his illness and their age had long curtailed such exotic adventures. But we loved listening to their story and, in my letter, I told her so. When I met her in the bank parking lot a few weeks later, she told me that my letter was a treasure. Several women told about their new approach to writing those difficult notes of sympathy: "For anyone who is widowed, I am much more likely to write that note and even to talk more intimately than I would have before." "I write saying how many of us have survived this painful experience and urge them to lean heavily on friends and family because this helps them feel needed. It's heartwarming to find out how many people really do care." "I have not had any friends become widowed since my husband died. Previously my comments had been clichés and generic, perhaps because I feared stirring up memories. I found, to the contrary, that I most cherished the notes that recalled certain events or characteristics in connection with my husband."

To close this chapter about friends, read what a woman in the six to ten year group has to say, "A surprising number—maybe a scandalous number—of my female friends are openly envious of my freedom and independence."

Readings suggested by women in the project include the following:

Willa Cather, *Death Comes for the Archbishop*
Daphne Du Maurier, *Without Him*
John KennethGalbreath, any writings about finances
Natalie Davis Ginsburg, *To Live Again*
Madelaine L'Engle, *Two-Part Invention*
Barbara Kingsolver, *Prodigal Summer*
C.S. Lewis, *A Grief Observed*
Sherwin B. Nuland, *How We Die*
Sylvia Porter, any writings about finances
V. Sackville-West, *All Passion Spent*
Scripture
LeoTolstoy, *The Death of Ivan Ilyich*
Francis Weaver, *Girls With Grandmother Faces*
Agnes Wilson, *The Middle Age of Mrs. Eliot*
Virginia Woolf, *To The Lighthouse*

6

⁓ Finances ⁓

During the reunion discussion at Smith College, Barbara Mulhern spoke about finances. She already had done research on the financial problems most women face at this difficult time. Although she knew that some women were prepared to handle whatever horrors might ensue, she realized there were others who were not, and still others who, even with some preparation, had not done or understood enough. With our project, she has been able to use her early work, hoping, as we all are, to encourage husbands and wives to deal openly with finances and to prepare for what is inevitable. The inevitability is that one of the spouses will die. We believe the stories our responders have shared are of vital importance to both the wives and the husbands who are going to face this separation

The subject of finances must be brought to the attention of women who are still married, and to the attention of their husbands. No matter the age of couples, whether younger, Baby Boomers or from the World War II generation, they should share and prepare. "No financial secrets" is a fine motto. "Make out your will, today" is another. The stories women told us about their experiences will prove this point. They also will help women who are facing the difficult financial decisions of early widowhood and need to learn, once more, that their problems are not unique.

Barbara Mulhern began her discussion at the Smith reunion with a frank assessment of a limitation of our project, saying that the replies have come from a small group of well-educated women. Most but not all of them are in the middle or upper income brackets. They have access to lawyers, accountants, brokers, trust funds, bankers, as well as interested and educated family members. From the outset, we assumed that many of these women and their husbands had made good financial plans. Much as we wished the opposite to be true, we knew that not all of them would have done this work, and that not every woman would have been involved in the financial decisions that now were vital to her survival. We are continually astonished and deeply concerned to hear from friends that "so and so's husband died, and she has no idea what their finances are, never had!" This is not generational. It's always wrong.

⪺ ⪺ ⪻ ⪻

"In going over the responses," Barbara Mulhern said, "I am not greatly surprised that the majority are positive. It is the negative ones that deserve our attention. But first, let me tell you what one woman reported. I believe it embodies the kindest thing any of us can do. This woman wrote, 'My husband had planned fully for his death. Every year he wrote and filed an *Adieu Letter* to his children and to me, an updated version, and he would gently chide me for not doing likewise. His letters were explicit in every area and a great help from Day One after he died. I have not yet written my own *Adieu Letter*, but this questionnaire may be the timely nudge I need.'" Barbara added that the project might be the timely nudge we all need. Several years have passed since the reunion and Barbara's report. The *Adieu Letter* still stands out among all the responses about planning.

⪺ ⪺ ⪻ ⪻

The questions we asked about finances are these. How did you and your husband prepare each other for an eventual death? How did the financial resolutions match your understanding of what would happen? In retrospect, do you wish you had done more by way of planning? What were the major financial difficulties you encountered following his death? What assistance did you receive? Was it valuable?

Sixty-seven women shared how they and their husbands planned, from a succinct, "We didn't," to lengthy details of what happened because they didn't, and stories of what they did so things ran smoothly.

⌒ ⌒ ⌒ ⌒

Helen's Story (First year, continued)

"During the first two or three days after Alan's diagnosis, we got a durable power of attorney in place. I encouraged Alan to make a list of all our assets. A few months later, our attorney conferred with us at Alan's bedside for a listing of the assets and expectations of costs for estate settlement. There was concern on my part as to what my responsibilities were going to be and how I would be able to manage them. Now, we believe estate settlement costs may not be as high as expected. Additional planning would have had to be done years earlier to have made some changes in investments.

"Difficulties? Nine months of Alan's illness and my constant care giving coupled with the final surrender to death. The hundreds of cards, flowers, etc., and endless mounds of paperwork and meetings plus business phone calls—monumental—leaving me exhausted. The accountants whom I enlisted became my islands of refuge. One female friend allowed me to use her assistance for understanding financial avenues unknown to me. A bank president and his wife were constantly on call, and I learned much from them and another friend in finances."

⌒ ⌒ ⌒ ⌒

Jane's Story (First year, continued)

"We had a will. Church service was authorized. I had control of all liquid assets. I had credit cards in my own name. I learned to do our federal (IRS) tax. I visited the undertaker a month before and made all the arrangements. Prepared an obituary. Local Social Security agent took care of all their requirements for me. Difficulties: the proliferation of Medicare statements. Discerning all the requirements: legal, medical, filing insurance claims. Social Security. Pension. Filing the will." In what Jane called an addendum she wrote, "I discovered only after John's death that our insurance policies, three of them, all carried a paragraph about the waiver of premiums in cases of permanent disability. We had continued to pay annual premiums for fifteen years. Now I am trying to recoup some of these payments—a very involved process."

Caroline's Story (First year, continued)

"Fortunately our affairs were in good order. After David collapsed two years ago, we rushed to finish our estate planning, get papers signed while he could still do that much. Everything was taken care of, and I'm grateful for that grace period which propelled us forward. No major financial difficulties. I have a good team of tax accountant, lawyer, investment counselor and broker. All have been valuable in processing the after-death matters and giving me advice."

Helen, Jane and Caroline, writing about their first year experiences, were joined by eleven other first year responders, several of whom spoke of planning with their husbands, and of the fact that they and he had worked together on their daily and future financial procedures. Helping us to stress our point about the importance of mutual responsibility, one woman said, "Since I handled the checkbook and bills, it made it easier. Other widows I know knew nothing regarding their finances!" From another woman, "He was in good health and in two months he was dead. We never made plans for either him or me, whoever died first. I guess we expected each other to face with courage whatever befell."

A couple of responses emphasize the truism that not everything can be done because we do not know when death will occur: "Shortly before he died, we had begun looking at methods to lower estate taxes and pass assets to the children. We had not completed this process. I wish we had started earlier!" "Unfortunately, final provisions for a life insurance policy remained in the formulation stage." The husband died suddenly. Another husband "did all that I would have expected from him in the year before he died. In preparing for his eventual complete retirement, he saw that everything was recorded in a black notebook. I am very grateful for this." From one of several whose financial situations were difficult, "The big problem I had was how to support myself and find a focus for my life! My husband left me with some life insurance, but I will have to work to support myself. It was not lack of planning, but financial disaster that caused the problem."

⌒ ⌒ ⌒ ⌒

Pat's Story (Second year, continued)

"We had planned for my independence should Peter die. My advisors insist that I am very well situated but, like many widows, I am fearful of being dependent on my children. I'm very cautious financially, but I think that is my nature. There were so many important decisions to make ALONE. Peter was my constant companion and advisor; no one could know me that well. Emotionally I was very vulnerable and really didn't want to make those decisions which actually were finalizing his death and my widowhood."

⌒ ⌒ ⌒ ⌒

Susan's Story (Second year, continued)

"I had an income of my own for fifteen years or so before William's death, so had sufficient money to handle everything financially while his estate was being settled. We did no specific planning, even when we both knew he was dying, largely because of my disinterest in financial matters. Although I had ample money, I did need the advice of a financial consultant and my lawyer, and later my stockbroker to help me with financial planning and management. Actually, I functioned much better in this area than I expected."

There are other responses from women in the second year. One wrote, "It would have been easier had financial concerns, especially plans for the future, been discussed between me and my husband and our financial advisor and attorney before the crises of his death." A woman who said she had always handled the finances of the family reported she had no problems, at least financially. The fifth woman in this group tells a different story, "Our income was cut in half. I received widow's benefits eight months later at age 60. I went back to work. I live quite modestly, self-supporting, but not too many frills. I see my friends in their golden years—it's tough for me! I rent out my home each spring to generate money to visit family. I am a good business manager. We had planned things well, very few difficulties. I have scaled down my expectations but still have massages, care of hair, care of self, and so on."

Many women in the three to five year group tell of previously shared financial responsibilities, others admit that there was little discussion. One woman reported that she was able to handle their situation without having been a financial partner, "My husband planned well, except for explaining income taxes carefully. I am learning successfully." Another wrote, "My husband showed me our records with enthusiasm and in great detail, and spent much valuable time showing me how to take over his desk and files." One not as successful but classic, "We have a good lawyer and we both had personal trusts. He had prepared a list of things to do financially and told me it was in his desk. Unfortunately, I did not find it for six months. I should have looked for the list before he died. Denial, again!"

Some told of difficulties: "He had no will, no directives for me. We didn't have our financial futures well planned at all." This woman did not write further about financial problems, so we assume and hope she made it through the maze. "Didn't prepare. I always knew about finances as I had inherited some money and managed it. He took over managing his, which gave me more time for my art. I had to spend much time—and still do—locating information, even though I set up a filing system in addition to his neatly arranged one."

⌒ ⌒ ⌒ ⌒

Jean's Story (Three to five years, continued)

"I had always handled our financial affairs, so this was not a problem for me. We made a deliberate decision to do this when we were first married. My attorney was very helpful, and both my sons are in the investment business, so when I need advice I can trust, it is available. We had planned reasonably well, possibly could have avoided some state taxes, but by and large, I had no problems. The difficulties I experienced were emotional, not practical. I have always been able— and still am—to take care of myself and deal with practical problems. Actually, it was helpful to me to have things to do and to figure out— it gave me a sense of pride that I could do this with no difficulty."

⌒ ⌒ ⌒ ⌒

Anne's Story (Three to five years, continued)

"Two years before his death, we made new wills, set up trusts. His business was already closed down, and we were well set up. I am very thankful for his care in these matters. I was an Executor of his will and, in the early nine months, I worked with the lawyer finding things in our files, writing letters, dealing with inquiries. This made me feel useful doing what he would want me to do. Now, I no longer feel I necessarily need to do what he would want. One of the advantages of being a widow is that you make the decisions for yourself. You run your life, and for me that is a heady feeling. I do find it difficult to face up to spending money in large amounts, as we always talked over our financial matters."

≈ ≈ ≈ ≈

A very wise woman wrote, "One thing I have done is to try to set up my affairs so when I die, the children will not be swamped. I've listed all financial holdings and indicated what heading each is found under in my file cabinet. I have inventoried furniture, jewelry, silver, etc., and I've done a Living Will and a Health Care Proxy. Now I can attend to the present!"

≈ ≈ ≈ ≈

Women from every group wrote about problems with Medicare procedures and doctor bills. From my own experience, the difficulty with both was enormous. I do not know how anyone without excellent financial skills can handle—let alone understand—the forms of Medicare. Are other insurance forms so difficult? Trying to keep forms and facts straight was nearly impossible. I soon decided never to cash a Medicare check. I signed all of them over to the clinic and the doctors. It worked for us.

≈ ≈ ≈ ≈

Katherine's Story (Three to five years, continued)

Katherine wrote, "As you see, we didn't!" Then she continued, "My brother is an attorney, though out of state, so I acted as Executrix of the estate with his advice. The only difficulties I encountered were the result of policies of our state's probate court deliberately designed so that you need a lawyer for a process actually simpler than filing a health insurance claim!"

⁓ ⁓ ⁓ ⁓

Karen's Story (Three to five years, continued)

"My husband and I differed greatly in our approach to money, so we always had separate accounts and never discussed finances. All except personal bills were paid through his office. I knew nothing of his financial affairs, nor did anyone else. Five and a half years later, I'm still trying to sort things out. I wish he had been given better advice. He rewrote his will shortly before he died, but it was poorly handled and cost the estate a lot of unnecessary taxes and fees. Dealing with the odds and ends of business and financial affairs was the most difficult thing I've had to cope with. I felt, and still feel, bitter towards lawyers who, I think, gave me bad advice, alienated my children and charged usurious fees. I really feel victimized by them and angry I wasn't smarter. A former partner of my husband's, who is my financial advisor, has been most helpful"

⁓ ⁓ ⁓ ⁓

Writing about her experience, another woman in the three to five year group says, "During his brief illness, he gave me a crash course in financial management. I had never handled household affairs. Never a mathematician, I was overwhelmed during those first months of learning the ropes! Budgeting, taxes, health insurance, etc., were foreign to me. My good friend and attorney referred me to a financial advisor who also became a sometime therapist, and to a woman tax consultant. These three people were my salvation throughout the emotionally charged first two years after my husband's death. I'm sorry I was so ill prepared in money matters. I'd been spared that responsibility—I'd been spoiled." What better way to bring out the idea that marriage and finance require women to learn, men to share—and vice versa? If you are close to any couples who have not made arrangements of partnering and sharing, take time to tell them about this woman's and so many other women's responses.

≈ ≈ ≈ ≈

Betsy, Judith and Beverly said they had no problems handling their finances. They and their husbands shared information and either made good plans or, in Betsy's case, she had always handled finances so experienced no difficulties except, as she wrote, "in the '$' area." Judith said that her major difficulty was "in getting life insurance companies to respond to my letters and return phone calls. My son, who came each weekend, helped me to write firmer letters!"

≈ ≈ ≈ ≈

Eight of the twenty-five responses from the six to ten year group specifically mention shared financial responsibilities. There may have been more sharing in this and other groups, but we took the responses literally in our assessments. If sharing was mentioned, we counted it. As in other groups, several said their husbands planned well. Even though we believe that most of our responders are not in financial distress, a few hinted that there was trouble. We did not ask for or expect intimate details. We respect one woman's candor, "We made wills and gave one another power of attorney. His life insurance was for his children, mine for him. We never had enough money to make the traditional financial plans. That didn't bother me and it still doesn't." Obviously, what they did was right for them.

Of the women in the six to ten year group who did not fare so well, one said, "I was not prepared to deal with investments and did not pay as much attention as I should have. I just didn't have the knowledge or the ability to concentrate on things like that. So I lost some money. Neither of us had wills, and in some states I could have lost the girls. In our state, it did not matter, fortunately. A point to be emphasized to all who have children, though." Another, "I understood nothing about financial problems. He tried to explain a little to me once but he always handled all this, so I didn't know much. I wish he had insisted that I know more." He? Or should she have insisted? Other women spoke proudly about how they and their husbands handled finances: "The financial planning was the smoothest. We had always handled everything together and talked together to our broker and lawyer. Our lawyer handled the settling of the estate. This was not a problem." "We planned enough. He had his pension fund and a life insurance trust. We both had a reasonably good idea of our financial status. Best of all, we had a fine system in household affairs. I wrote the checks and he signed them, so we both knew where the money went." Although this report is very positive, I find myself wondering if she also could have signed their checks. Undoubtedly this is because I have known two women who were not permitted to have access to checking accounts.

Other stories from the six to ten year group: "Unlike some, we talked about it a great deal. We talked less about financial decisions than philosophically about how to raise the children, how I would cope, that I should take off my rings, I should remarry. He gave me great freedom. All the financial questions sorted themselves out better than I could have imagined. I had to make very few changes. More planning would have been wiser. I was probably lucky." "He had all his affairs in perfect order as he knew he was living on borrowed time. With the aid of my lawyer, his estate was settled in no time. My first husband's estate took four and a half years even though his affairs were in order, too." One story from this group gives us warning of what can happen, "His insurance helped me. My will would have helped him. The Living Trust helped his children, but put me on the fence for about three years. His estate was only closed after six years because of tiny, sophisticated investments that were tangled. Also, one of his business partners wouldn't acknowledge money from insurance as being due me. Had to reach a settlement. Personal friend, his lawyer, resolved it for a large charge." Two women in this group handled the matter of finances themselves, one not too well: "I am a librarian and it was easy for me to dig out some of the answers to my own questions. I read tons!" "Making out health insurance claims was overwhelming. A neighbor who had been a banker offered to help, but I kept thinking, 'I can do this myself!' I should have accepted the help. Though, perhaps, it was good that it kept me busy for months!" Other reports: "I was pressured into making decisions too quickly. Had I waited and worked with someone less commission driven, I would be far better off today." "The main difficulty I had was dealing with the bank account. Towards the end, he realized he hadn't done more with me on this and wished he had." "The major difficulty was feeling I was unprepared to deal with investments. I had always handled the checkbook and paid the bills, but the larger issues and amounts were something I had never had to deal with. I trusted too much a friend in the insurance business!" Larger amounts were troubling to more than one, particularly because decisions about these had to be made alone. Often the first major decision is to purchase a car. Selling the house figures in some responses as does buying another. Life goes on. We can learn from mistakes. Connie said that widows are brave. We have to be.

⇒ ⇒ ⇐ ⇐

Stephanie's Story (More than ten years, continued)

"My husband handled our finances. But I listened and asked questions. One of the areas that surprised me was how knowledgeable I had become. After my husband's death, I asked a friend, a professor at the business school, for a book about finances—meanings of words, descriptions of equities, and so on. In this way I felt more knowledgeable when I talked with our lawyer, with the trust officials, with a financial advisor."

⇒ ⇒ ⇐ ⇐

Connie's Story (More than ten years, continued)

"I wish I had more widow-training in financial matters.

However, a good banker in trust funds and an old friend, the family lawyer, spoke to me as if I was ten years old, and I soon caught on. My oldest son was invaluable. He created files, folders and habits which I still follow. I really had no major difficulties."

⌒ ⌒ ⌒ ⌒

At the Smith College reunion discussion, we were astonished when one woman said she and her husband had not yet drawn up wills, although he practiced in law and jurisprudence. Later, her questionnaire revealed that, even with the best of intentions, he never did complete the document.

When the plans my husband and I made with our lawyer became reality, I found myself wishing I had listened more carefully, known better or been told exactly what would happen in greater detail. The plans were fine, but it turned out they were complicated in ways I had not expected. Jerry and I always discussed everything, always met jointly with our lawyer and stockbroker. We were in agreement concerning finances, wills, financial hopes and expectations. However, because of New Mexico laws, and the fact that our investments were held in "joint tenancy with right of survivorship," we had to call in the lawyer and friends to witness transfers of stock from that holding to "joint tenancy." This just two days before Jerry died. He was up and able to sign; our stockbroker daughter explained the reasons. Had we not made this change, parts of the settlement would have been much less helpful to me. (Along with several others, New Mexico is a community property state. Rules and regulations are different here.) When I met with the lawyer after Jerry died, I discovered that I had not clearly understood what would happen, especially with the spousal trust which, according to daughter Elizabeth, I regard as an enemy. It does take managing and understanding, and, I also found, is treated differently by different accountants. After four tries, I have found both a lawyer and an accountant with whom I communicate well. Together, we have solved the prickly problems.

The next big step for me was to draw up my own will, a process I found much more difficult than the experience we had together when Jerry was alive. With this new instrument, I had to understand what would happen because I had to make all the decisions myself. I feel free to make changes if I wish, or if changing financial markets require me to do so. Still, I carry some concerns about fairness and "is that enough?" when I consider children, friends, institutions and gifts. As someone said, the ideal is to spend all your money before you die. Who can tell when to do it, if that really is the goal?

Checking back again in the journal pages I wrote during the first and second years, I was startled to see how often I mentioned my financial concerns even though at the time I knew, deep down, that I would not have a serious problem in this area. Still, I worried. If you ask other women or their families about this continuing concern and the accompanying need for reassurance, you will find both occur very often.

⁂

In her reunion discussion, Barbara gave hero recognition to a woman who is in the more than ten years group. She wrote, "I read as many simplified books on finance as I could: Sylvia Porter, Galbreath, etc. Took a course on personal finance and got opinions from as many people as possible. Diversified my holdings and put the bulk with a good brokerage. My helpful brother-in-law said, 'Get a good advisor and don't worry your pretty little head!' That I ignored!"

Other women in this same group spoke of problems with medical insurance, bad experiences, bad memories that do not go away. Several women found adequate help or had already been involved with competent professionals. One woman wrote of serious difficulties following the deaths of both her first and her second husbands. She told of technical problems with the will and with IRS decisions, with years in probate court, loss, financial misuse by her husband's brother, misunderstandings about pension and life insurance. She added, "Thanks to good attorneys, the pension was preserved, but again, life insurance—term insurance—was denied. Another time, even if it seems inconvenient or overly assertive at a time of termination, I would seek legal counsel and be sure to have everything in writing!"

Ingenuity, independence and a strong sense of self abound in the stories of two women who handled aspects of their financial situations differently from most: "I settled my husband's estate with the local clerk of the court. I did not need a lawyer. It was time consuming but not difficult, and there were no snags. It gave me enormous self-confidence for handling future affairs." "The first thing that had to be done was to probate the will. We had never gotten a lawyer up here, so I went to town hall. The probate judge and her assistant, both women, encouraged me to do it myself. So I did. Their confidence set me off. It was great. Since then, both they and I have encouraged other women to try, to read and to become involved even if and when they go to a lawyer and/or financial advisor."

⌒ ⌒ ⌒ ⌒

Here are some suggestions that will serve people well in dealing with finances and expectations. You might pass them on to friends newly widowed or still married:

- Remember that some insurance companies would rather retain the principle "as an investment for you" than pay it out. Be firm about your wishes.
- Ask the mortician for at least twenty-five copies of the death certificate. Get Letters of Testamentary or whatever else you might need—ask—from your city or county clerk.
- If you write the obituary, let the mortuary make newspaper arrangements.
- Where is your marriage certificate? You will need the original for Social Security settlements.

- Do you both know what is in your safety deposit box at the bank? Check it out often. It may hold papers of importance, or things that will become part of the estate.
- Do your lawyers, accountants and stockbrokers know the financial specifics of your state of residence? There can be ticklish problems if they do not.
- Do you each have credit cards in your own name?
- Whose name is on the title to the house and the car? Is that what you both want?
- Do you each know what is going on in your financial lives? Are your accounts jointly held?
- Are we correct in assuming that each of you has made your will?
- Today is a good time to write your first *Adieu Letter*!

7

☙Society☙
Out and About

Questions: How did you manage your re-entry into the social scene? What situations were difficult for you? How did you think society looked at you? Do you still have that opinion? What name do you use? What advice do you have? These are the subjects that occupy this chapter. We wanted to know how our people coped with being single in the big, big world that has stayed the same while they and their life styles have changed immeasurably. What awaits the new widow when she strikes out on her own? Obviously her relation to her community is important. If she has lived in the same town since birth, friendships are deep, reaching back to childhood. She knows everyone. She should be included. But she is not the same person in the same relationship. The community's perspective of her will have changed. Her perspective of herself will have changed, also.

Three months after Jerry McNally died, I needed to order new personal stationery. This time, I decided the letterhead would read "Shirley Reeser McNally" instead of "Mrs. James Jerome McNally." Abandoning my married name made me both sad and guilty but I realized "Mrs. JJM" was a statement of who I had been rather than who I now would have to become. For me, this was a sensible and correct decision. In their responses, some agreed, others did not.

The problems of title, name, label, by choice or error, have continued to interest me. Despite my decision to be "Shirley Reeser McNally," people insist on addressing letters or listing my name with a title, albeit an erroneous one: "Mrs." That combination indicates I am divorced. Then there is "Ms." Women in my generation, even those who are strongly feminist, seem to avoid this designation. Younger women to whom I have spoken do not share our dislike. An attorney friend says she prefers "Ms" because she believes a female title should be no more revealing than the male "Mr." "Why should my title indicate my marital status, something that is no one's business?" is her question. "'Ms' is a generational thing," another younger woman said. I realize my name with no title is difficult for some people to use with my address, but it's fine with me. I use the non-titled three-word name when I write to my widowed friends although I notice that some of them still use their married names. One woman in the project said she introduces herself as Jane Wright Simpson but wants to see Mrs. John Simpson on any letters she receives. Another woman admitted she uses her married name when she feels "more clout is appropriate." Many of us do that.

～ ～ ～ ～

In this present day of informality and introductions lacking last names, I do not appreciate "Shirley" and always say, "I'm Shirley McNally." Conversely, I want to be "Mrs. McNally" at the X-ray lab or the doctor's but know that won't happen unless I'm trading with an upscale office where my preference for "Mrs. McNally" will be established on day one. Like many of our responders, I do not use the label "widow." I don't care much for "single" but must accept it. In a conversation where marital status becomes of interest, I avoid any euphemisms and say that my husband died several years ago. One woman in the project wrote that how we regard and speak of ourselves may well be one of our most important decisions.

≈ ≈ ≈ ≈

Our local newspaper, *The New Mexican*, runs a daily column entitled "The Past 100 Years." This piece appeared in 1991 when we were in the earliest stages of the project. Dated November 7, 1891, it announced, "Mrs. Jefferson Davis, a relic of the Southern Confederacy's presidency, passed though Lamy yesterday en route east from Mexico." (Jefferson Davis had died in 1889.)

Not only is this woman denied a name of her own, she is related to an office. While the description of her as a relic is in use occasionally—I have come across it twice, both times referring to women—it tends to reduce Mrs. Davis to a bone or a hank of hair. According to the newspaper, Varine Howell Davis was not much of a person in her own right, although she had been an accomplished hostess with fine-tuned political skills and was a published author. But she did travel to Mexico leading, we might assume, an entourage of companions and servants. We also might assume that her status as a widow is what permitted her to undertake the journey. And probably she wore black from head to toe. At least it was autumn.

≈ ≈ ≈ ≈

Early on, we asked whether some sort of mourning dress might make life easier for us. It would define our situation immediately and obviate the need for any explanations. A response from one woman suggested that a black mourning ring might be helpful. Antique mourning jewelry is highly collectible today, but I suspect the average observer would not recognize what such a ring or brooch signifies.

Wedding rings are a different matter, much discussed. As a symbol of our marriage, and because I liked them, I continued to wear my wedding and engagement rings for several years, wondering when it would be appropriate and emotionally sound for me to take them off. If there are protocols for this, I am unaware of them. Actually, the decision was made for me. My engagement ring, an antique family piece, had been strengthened and repaired many times until it became too fragile to wear. I put it and my wedding ring in a safe place and bought a new piece that makes no statement except, I hope, one of style. It's a big ring; I'm happy with it. My college roommate wears her wedding and engagement rings on her right hand. One woman in the project says this is her solution, also. A friend had her own wedding band and her husband's set one inside the other. She wears them on a gold chain. Whatever each woman chooses to do is her own business. If it makes her feel better, more secure, if it solves a problem, so be it.

⤚ ⤚ ⤙ ⤙

For a lot of years I wore my gray hair in a Santa Fe ponytail, sometimes up, sometimes down. The year after Jerry died, my hairdresser convinced me to let her cut my hair short and dye it red. I loved it! Two years later, we decided I would go blond. Then, when a four-year-old child asked me if I was wearing a wig, I went right back to my own gray. Now quite white, I am enjoying really good hair days. A nice bonus. No one in Santa Fe remembers what color I used to be, but I must admit that the adventure of red hair helped me feel like a new person at a time when that was important.

⤚ ⤚ ⤙ ⤙

During the early stages of re-entry into the social scene, women may run into some difficulties even if they have lived in their community for years. Obviously, women new to a community will have more problems. Both need friends to support them. The majority of women in the project reported that they found being with friends at small parties was "do-able" in the early stages. They also reported that being single in larger gatherings was not easy.

A woman in the first year tells us she is learning to face being on her own but "I do not want to be considered a fifth wheel. I am well aware that the world moves in couples, so I try not to force myself on any group."

Statements about being a "fifth wheel" and not wanting to invade a couple's group are part of the widow's litany. Fifth wheel fears loom large. Self worth can diminish during the early months of widowhood. Exclusion from the couple's world may be more imagined than actual, but the thought of it is hurtful. However, for us, a shift has occurred. Now we spend more time with the wives, less time with the couples—more time during the days, less time in the evenings. And, for many, less time on the weekends. Except for those who are determined to marry again, most of us find that we are becoming more open to new friendships with other single women who, like ourselves, are constructing their own new communities apart from the couple's world we used to inhabit.

There have always been communities separate from the married ones we knew. Widows eventually find—or "found"—a community that works well for them. Women who have never married construct their own. (How often did any of us who were married wonder how these women dealt with their solitary status?) Women who have been divorced form communities. Women who have relationships that may or may not lead to marriage function in a community not entirely separate from the couple's world, but it is different. Communities are not always specific to any one life style; they may draw from a wide variety of people, yet the majority of members share the same life situations.

Today, sociologists are watching with interest a trend among mature women to join together—to team up—to make what can be called a kind of family. These women decide to live together, independently and truly in the sense of sisters. They team up perhaps because of finances, certainly because they are tired of living alone. They often go to social functions together. They share what they wish of their lives. They construct their family atmosphere for companionship and for practical reasons beyond friendship. "I could never share a kitchen with another women" is being replaced by "Why do we want to rattle around alone in our houses?" If it can work, it's a fine solution to a lot of the problems of being single, particularly the constancy of loneliness. As two friends of mine who are doing this successfully tell me, you have to be very sure of who you are, you really have to love and admire each other, and you have to ignore a lot of misunderstanding on the part of other people. You also have to be brave enough to leave the familiar and concentrate on the future. Under any circumstances, this last is what widows must do.

⇌ ⇌ ⇌ ⇌

Helen's Story (First year, continued)

"I'm soon going into my fourth month of loss. There are a few social occasions I can talk about. Two months after we lost Alan, I was invited to a cultural community event. The invitation arrived in my name. My name appeared on the program as Mrs. Alan Blair. That was thundering! But it also began to give me a sense of my oneness and independence. Many, many friends whom I had not seen gathered around me. The attention was overwhelming and gratifying. My sense is that some felt deep compassion, some were sorry for me, and many felt that I had great courage and so offered much respect for me and the ordeal I had to and am taking in hand.

"Alan and I almost always traveled and attended functions together. I do hold my own in functions now, and I'm able to travel alone. Opportunities to attend functions do not present themselves often. Travel for the time being is minimal due to current other costs that I have incurred. One small trip found me fretting over having to drive myself to the airport, park the car and lug the suitcases. It also made me appreciate the fact that I had once been well looked after and taken care of. Determination then began to set in place."

Helen said when she meets people she gives her name as Helen Blair, mentions where she lives and, if the situation merits, she says that her husband was the comptroller of a small university and "I lost him four months ago."

≈ ≈ ≈ ≈

Jane's Story (First year, continued)

Jane reported that, as the wife of a priest, she was often on her own in social situations, especially ones in which John played an official role: teaching, preaching, speaking, weddings, funerals, etc. "I have no problem in doing things alone. I will go out alone rather than give up outside activities." As far as meeting new people, she says, "I introduce myself as Jane Porter. My daughter and one daughter-in-law retained their maiden names. I feel comfortable with Jane Porter instead of the Mrs. John Porter I used before."

≈ ≈ ≈ ≈

Caroline reminded us that it has not been quite three months, so she's feeling her way, "I am very comfortable with old friends. When David was alive, we traveled and attended social events together. I did not do much alone. I will have to try it."

≈ ≈ ≈ ≈

Other women in the first year group: "I was comfortable being with friends—couples and singles—but did not put myself in the situation of large group gatherings where I knew I'd feel alone and awkward." "After a while, I felt that it was more difficult for some friends: when they see me, they still tend to look past me for him." "I'm all right in most social situations where we were known, except in church. I still cannot stand the place. In new situations, I'm fine. I've made several wonderful new friends (females and couples) recently. My regret is that he didn't know these people."

≈ ≈ ≈ ≈

Pat's Story (Second year, continued)

Writing of her experiences as she took the steps that started her return to the social scene, she told us, "I did better in situations where I was not known, and therefore somewhat anonymous. When I could be Pat Williams, it was infinitely easier than when I was Peter Williams' widow, and I believe that people reacted/react to me differently."

≈ ≈ ≈ ≈

Susan's Story (Second year, continued)

Susan has more to say than Pat, and she takes exception to my dislike of the word "widow."

"I at first felt like a fifth wheel with married friends but got over that. I'm just glad now to be included. Going to events alone, particularly where I'm not well known, is lonely and difficult but gives me a stronger sense of self than when William was alive. I have had no problems being accepted and included.

"Occasionally William and I went to Cape Cod separately, and one year he took a southern tour by himself, but for the most part we did things together. I have never had a problem being alone. I enjoy functioning as an independent person, not that I would have chosen to be alone all the time, as I now must. When I meet people and want to say who I am, I say I am a widow and a priest, mother and grandmother. In my opinion, 'widow' has a centuries-old tradition of being a term of respect and compassion. It has dignity. The Bible is full of exhortations to care for the widowed."

≈ ≈ ≈ ≈

Another second year response, "The transition over the first two years was difficult. I felt that I had been cast out so quickly, and not for anything I had done. I also found that many single and divorced women did not want me as a part of their groups because I was not divorced. As a young widow, I found myself in a very strange and lonely place, with no examples to follow and no proper place to fit in. I have adjusted in some ways to this but still resent that I am somehow considered to be only on the fringes of normalcy."

No one can downplay the tragedy of early widowhood. Without negating any of the comments from this young woman, I find myself wondering how disrupting her situation was to her friends and her social community. "Normal" in the adult society where most of us lived, involves husbands and wives—couples. Now, most of us seem to exist on the fringes of the couple society. As time goes on, many of us may find that this edgy location is very pleasant, our view of life is good. Being on the edge leads to new adventure. Going into new territory means leaving the old behind, but we take our memories with us.

～ ～ ～ ～

It has occurred to me and to several friends that there have been occasions when we can admit we are glad our husbands did not live long enough to suffer the debilitation and sorrow old age can bring. Sympathy for those having to endure this distress is unbounded. We agree, also, that we are glad that we did not have to fall prey to the argumentative life styles adopted by so many couples as they age from the sixties to the seventies and into the eighties with these ever-increasing physical and, sometimes, mental frustrations. I am astonished to hear couples argue harshly in what seems to be their only method of communication. I'm saddened to watch as one takes what has become a kind of parental control. I suspect these people have become so used to this behavior they do not notice what has happened. I admit I have become judgmental about still-married friends and acquaintances who, it seems to me, are not taking advantage of the precious time left to them. I also am sad to see the suffering that old age brings to so many. I rejoice with those whose health, both physical and mental, remains strong.

～ ～ ～ ～

Jean's Story (Three to five years, continued)

"I was, and still am, most comfortable in social situations where I am well known. At first, I tried to go into situations where I was not known and it was miserable, so I have stopped doing this except where there is a particular reason, usually business, to go. It was not a question of how society looked at me. I simply wasn't comfortable as a single woman. When we were married, I attended functions alone but did not travel without my husband. Now I only travel alone on business or with a particular destination, i.e., to visit someone. This is a matter of personal preference, having nothing to do with being married or single. Having been a widow for four years now, I only attend social functions where I am reasonably certain I will feel at ease and enjoy myself, which provides me with a more than adequate social life."

Ann's Story (Three to five years, continued)

"I am not entirely easy in mixed company. It's strange but true that there is a lot of difference between socializing when people know you have a husband even though he may not be there at the moment, and people knowing you are a widow. Most people don't know how to deal with widows. As for my going alone when Richard was alive, I didn't do that. We did things together. I don't particularly enjoy traveling alone but do it to visit my two distant children. There is one child still near enough, so I can drive there. I take some pleasure in being able to get to an airport 100 miles away, park in the long-term lot, get myself onto a plane and then home again. But it isn't the fun traveling used to be.

"Social events are difficult for me to face up to, especially dinner parties. I've had lots of houseguests, but no male and female dinner parties. Women to lunch, however. I hate walking into a party alone."

Katherine's Story (Three to five years, continued)

"Because I married late and had a continuing career, I always had a separate professional and social identity and often traveled and went to functions alone, so I don't think the perception of me has changed."

By now, you have noticed that the women who, like Katherine, had a continuing career are able to achieve some degree of comfort in the social arena almost from the beginning of their new situations. Without doubt, a career experience is extremely valuable in more ways than the earning of money. Some of our responders married at an early age and did not work for pay during the married years. They were volunteers. Is it the achievement or the paycheck that makes the difference? Success in the non-profit world does not bring the immediate acclaim afforded success in the business world, but volunteering is what keeps our communities alive—and it is, historically, the business of women. Our culture depends on volunteers: the arts, education, health are as dependent on donated hours as on donated funds, though, again, the check usually gets more applause than the time sheet. The paycheck provides a great sense of assurance and self-worth, but the successes of volunteering and its independence also bring a large measure of these. Women long active in either field have already developed great self-confidence and assurance. These become strong motivating factors in the healing process.

Karen's Story (Three to five years, continued)

"I avoided social contacts other than family or very close friends for several months, then suffered through months of making myself go to parties, trying not to be a wet blanket. It took me well over a year before I could drum up enough courage to do any entertaining. I never went anywhere I was not known. I felt society was sympathetic. I never did anything or went anywhere alone while I was married. After I'd been widowed, I felt very insecure trying to do things alone that I had done easily before I was married. After being so dependent, it was hard to change. My family helped until I could face traveling alone and also found single friends to do things with."

Although the word "dependent" is not one I would choose, I can say that Jerry's and my married life certainly was based on a special togetherness. We did depend on each other, every day. Before we were married, I enjoyed an interesting business life starting with the Executive Training Squad at R. H. Macy's in New York City. While the experience and training were invaluable, the retail field, at that time in my life, was not for me. I moved on to Street & Smith Publications in an editing and writing capacity, and then to CBS Television when shows were "live" and color was just coming in. A fascinating time that also included the McCarthy years—memorable and terrifying. My paycheck at CBS came from the writing group, but my work was as associate producer of the first woman's daytime CBS-TV network show, entitled *Vanity Fair*. When that show was cancelled, I joined *The Garry Moore Daytime Show*, still "live," still exciting, still fascinating, but I missed writing and, more important, I had met Jerry McNally who also worked at CBS. Marriage, then a home in the country and two children. I was busy in the community and deeply involved in the children's school projects. Jerry's many business commitments often took him away. Living in Connecticut, and later just outside New York, he took the train to the big city while I stayed home with the children. We were representative of so many families in the late 1950s and 1960s. We were suburbanites with a commuting husband who left home early, returned late, and with a wife who was expected to love the house, the schools, the community and the life that was prescribed in *Ladies Home Journal*, *McCall's* and *Good Housekeeping* magazines.

Once the children were out of elementary school, we decided—took the risk is more like it—to leave the New York commuter life and work at home, developing something we could do together. We spent the next seventeen years in our own business. We officed together, traveled together, wrote books and films together, fought and laughed together, and together we created a successful program called "Let's Learn Language" to develop the oral skills of young children who needed to learn English as a second language. We moved our family from Westchester, New York, to Washington, D.C. for business purposes. When our children became college students, we moved the family to Santa Fe, New Mexico, still in business, still working together.

A few years later, we shut down the business and retired. During Jerry's illness, we were together constantly, by necessity and inclination. Certainly we were dependent on each other. When he died, I needed my children's help, and I needed friends—the ones who stayed with us and the new ones who were to come. I believe the new friendships were vital to my survival and my growth. I believe this for all widows. New friendships are particularly necessary if we are among the first in our group to be widowed. If we are wise and fortunate, we will renew former friendships whenever we can. I have been astounded and thrilled by the happy renewal of relationships with many friends I knew before I was married: childhood friends, school friends and especially college friends. These Smith women remind me of who I once was and strengthen who I am now. Having shared what were very formative years for all of us, we now have a sense of sharing, once again, another time in our lives that is extremely formative and that, despite our sorrows, can be both rewarding and productive.

~ ~ ~ ~

Betsy's Story (Six to ten years, continued)

Remembering her experiences as she moved back into the social scene, Betsy wrote, "Reaction was varied. It was painful if it had been something we had done together; then sometimes I felt uncomfortable, almost defective. I hated the word 'widow' and at 52 felt I was much too young. Today, I am less concerned with what society thinks. I feel comfortable in most everything I do. As a working person, I did a fair amount alone. As a widow, I travel on business or with a national church board I serve on. I entertain couples, but find I am infrequently asked back, especially dinner parties that are couple oriented."

≈ ≈ ≈ ≈

Judith's Story (Six to ten years, continued)

"I did not mind going alone and really do not know if people minded my being at social functions alone. I did live in an area where there were many widows, which helped. When I was married, I had often traveled alone, so that did not bother me."

≈ ≈ ≈ ≈

Beverly's Story (Six to ten years, continued)

"I had always been the 'helper' not the 'helpee' so I felt uncomfortable having to deal with questions, comments and expressions of sympathy where I was known. I was glad to get away to where I was not known at times, so I could be treated like everyone else. I was viewed as brave, competent and perhaps 'too unemotional' for some who expected me to be a tragic figure. I had always been independent and did things on my own, as well as being part of a couple who valued our togetherness above almost all else. My new status made little change in those situations."

≈ ≈ ≈ ≈

A response from another woman with six to ten years' experience of living a single life tells how she managed in social situations. Like others, she brings new and interesting observations, "Where I was known, I knew I would be surrounded by kindness and concern, that my husband would still be somehow present for me and our friends, and I was glad to go. Where I was not known, I was just myself. Although I never thought how society might be looking at me, somewhere along the line I saw that a widow in a small or closely-knit society could throw things off. The social order is disturbed. A death disrupts, in every event. I understood why, for example, a widow might be stoned or driven out of a village in older or more primitive cultures. I know there are vestiges of this in ours, but my understanding was not forced on me by society. My widowhood no longer gives me special privileges nor does it evoke any disturbing emotions in and of itself. Clearly, this has something to do with the way I see myself. Curiously, I feel much less protected now than I did at first."

"Special privileges" of widowhood was a new term for us. People, some people, do take extra time to care for early widows. Some understand their vulnerability, recognize that they are newly different, not by choice, and that they are often "not themselves." This is how I understand her comments. You may see them differently. Friends show their concern, of course, as does family. Do we expect that little leeway because we are experiencing such a difficult time? I suspect we do. Whether we get it, and how long it continues, might depend on how well others understand our predicament.

⌒ ⌒ ⌒ ⌒

Stephanie's Story (More than ten years, continued)
"I hated parties. I still do. I felt that people felt sorry for me, but that was projection. As I have become more comfortable with my own identity, social situations are easier. I've developed some poise in walking into a room alone. But I still haven't overcome my

reluctance to give parties. I hate planning them alone; I hate the silence after the last guest leaves. In my married years, my husband and I traveled together, attended functions as a pair. In any of these situations, I still miss him. I cannot look across the room and see him smile at me!"

⤐ ⤐ ⤏ ⤏

Connie's Story (More than ten years, continued)

"Finally, in that first year, when I got hold of myself, I was indeed glad to socialize. My friends looked at me as they always had. I never had trouble with strangers. I was very independent when married. My husband traveled abroad a great deal, and when we lived abroad—seven years in Switzerland and seventeen in Japan—he didn't travel for pleasure. But I did, so I was easily able to adjust to traveling alone, going out alone. I had always made the travel plans for the family, in fact, I made most of our plans."

⤐ ⤐ ⤏ ⤏

Women who have traveled extensively and women who have lived abroad can be added to those busy professional and volunteering women who are out and about, used to attending large functions alone. Doctors' wives also have had considerable practice in this area. One very busy woman reports, "My own schedule of lecturing all across the country was already set up, so I simply continued my normal societal relations. However, in ordinary life, a single man is always more acceptable than a single woman. I am glad I live in a city where social gatherings are not necessarily geared to couples"

Is there anyone who is not affected by the social requirement to "pair?" And by the love of even numbers, the necessity for boy-girl seating? Women make the rules; women suffer because of them. Or does society call the shots? And who is society? I have moments of discomfort when I see that everyone else is paired with a mate or a partner, or when I know I am not included because I have neither, and my being there would make the numbers uneven. Actually, I no longer care about events where two are required. As the woman quoted last said, she lives in a city where social gatherings are not necessarily geared to couples. As I said earlier, I do, too, though occasionally I run into a married couple unaware of this fact.

Santa Fe is known for its strong women. Perhaps I am on my way to becoming one of them. I have no real problem attending events by myself. If it's important to me, I'll go. I prefer to go with a friend, but the unavailability of one will not keep me away. And I can always leave if I'm not having a good time. I have had a lot of experience with fundraising events, so I do have a problem when invitations include a better ticket cost for couples but I am cheered by the recognition, in my city, that any two people, whatever the relationship or gender, fall within the couple category.

It is always a happy occasion when a male friend and I have tickets to a concert, play or opera, and we decide to go together. Observers may make more of this by moving the definition of "friendship" toward "date." Perhaps it is only my generation that looks with future expectations on every male-female outing in public, a leftover from our early years when we dated and dating immediately suggested romance, even marriage. Of course, the absence of males in the older generation's community makes any possibility of a link titillating. For those interested in joining the game, the competition can be fierce.

The conviction that, in society, single men are more desirable than single women is prevalent throughout the responses. Most if not all of us regard this as absolute fact. We may not like it. We may want to suspect the depth of their grieving, to say, "Look here, men remarry quickly. They must have less of a problem with being widowed. They seem to get over it sooner." Or we might ask, "How do they really feel about being single? They do so well in the social world. The few available men are wined, dined and sought after while the many available women are home alone."

Pursuing interest in the comparison of men and women, we asked the following questions: Do you think men and women face the same problems after the death of the spouse? What similarities? What differences? On what do you base your conclusions?"

Women in the first year say: "I can't imagine it would be much different. Financial decisions might come more easily, but many men wouldn't know how to wash their clothes." "I think men are lost without a spouse. Women have all the household details to keep them busy, but how does a man manage? I think he should find a female companion—perhaps even marry again." "I think men not only lose a companion, but a provider of creature comforts. Because they have usually been exempt from the details of daily maintenance, they are twice bereaved, and this is especially demoralizing when their self-confidence is undermined." "In general, widowers seem needier than widows." "I feel men have an even tougher time." "Surely, grief is an equal-opportunity experience. However, I suspect that because many men have been conditioned to repress their emotions, the healing process may be inhibited." "They seem to find coming home to an empty house especially hard, based on several men's expectations in the widowed group I'm in. Also, the public expects them to be strong, and they may not get as much support as women do." "Most of the widowers I know are unhappy being alone. They really don't like it. And a lot get married again, soon. Women seem to adapt better, and the home base is comfortable to them, even if they are alone." "Men have a very difficult time, of a different sort. My generation of men was used to being taken care of at home. They face a new set of problems. They are free, however, to find a date; they travel easily. I find men to be far less able to cope with being alone."

≈ ≈ ≈ ≈

When my mother died at 57, my father went through difficulties I did not understand. I came home to live with him for the first year but I still worked in New York City and I was still single. It was obvious to me that the daily commute and isolation from my friends was not good. I realized that I had to move back into the city. During our discussions about how my father would respond to this change—he did not want to join me in New York—he told me his most difficult days were always Sundays. In the early years after Jerry died, these also were my most difficult days. I suspect both men and women mark Sunday afternoons and evenings as the loneliest times of the week. I spend them at the computer, reading the paper, listening to the news. I do not know how my father spent these times, or how other men get through them. I am sure it is not easy for any of us, no longer married, to fill the long Sunday hours we now spend at home alone but once spent at home alone, together.

◠ ◠ ◡ ◡

Writing their thoughts about widowers, women in the second year group said: "I think women are better able to cope. We are greater realists and more skilled at accepting change as part of life because of our biological natures: monthly changes, pregnancy, childbirth, etc. Widowers tend to remarry sooner. They don't know how to nurture themselves." "Men are less able to take care of themselves. But they can reach out for female companionship—not much male companionship around for a 61 year old, and how I do miss it."

From the three to five year group: "My observation is that men immediately seek—and usually find—a new relationship. Also, from my observation, most men cannot, and don't even try to survive on their own. Women can do this and usually successfully." "I have only compared notes with one widower. He said he was inundated with casseroles and invitations to dinner from widows. It really got to be a nuisance! I have invited no widowers, nor cooked any casseroles." "Men are often more lost, more helpless after the death of a spouse than women." "Do think many don't know what to do with themselves, yet don't have the guts to get up and go out and seek entertainment." "The need for congenial companionship is similar for widows or widowers, I believe. But a man's need may be greater because of a physical need, besides." "Men miss a housekeeper, laundress, cook and bedmate. Women miss a bedmate and escort. Men seem to hurry and remarry within a year or two. I am enjoying my independence and don't want to give it up for anyone."

From the six to ten year group: "Men face exactly the same emotional problems and many of the same social problems. I can hardly think of differences except that they are more sought after in a world where there are fewer men than women. Men are no less lonely, care no less to dine out alone. They are no happier without a beloved person alongside every night. I base this on the experience of good friends who had lost their wives and shared their grief and then comforted me in mine. Age made no difference." "I think men are more devastated, more likely to remarry on the rebound. They are less likely to acknowledge the importance of the grief process, join support groups, etc. I have spent a great deal of time with grieving men, and they all say these things. Support group statistics bear out these observations." "Loneliness is the same, but men usually have many people, including single women, who look after them. If he is the independent kind who is used to looking after a house or apartment and his own needs, it will be easier for him. Men have much fewer, if any, financial problems. I have known a few who remarry immediately, and others who wait a few years, but I really think it's much easier for men than for us." "At first I resented single men as more socially attractive. Now I know they have depended on their wives far more than they realized, and are lost. They've never been at home alone. It's too quiet there!" "Both my sisters died, and I think my brothers-in-law had more difficult times than I. Happily, each has remarried." "Thank goodness, just like each woman, each man is different. Each reacts to problems in his own unique way, including the death of his spouse. This is based on intimate experiences with three very different, very special widowers I have known—my second father, my second and third husbands."

A woman who writes from her perspective of more than ten years says she believes men have more problems than women. "Men face worse problems in a way. How to cope with daily tasks, meals, housekeeping, etc. But more males don't stay single very long!" Not one of the responses from any group indicates a conviction that men do not experience the same trauma, despair and terror that women do when the spouse dies. In reading the responses, one might say this part of grief is generic. The differences occur as time passes, when women agree, sadly but with good reason, that single men are much more socially acceptable than single women; indeed, men are more looked for, more desirable and certainly more pursued. From my own vantage point of more than ten years, I would ask the same questions I asked earlier: who makes the social rules, who does the party-planning, who accedes to the cultural requirements of boy-girl pairing that refuse to become archaic? Women. Married women. The social arbiters. Again, consider the women who have never married. Where do they fit into the social pattern? Also, consider that it is more culturally acceptable for women to be single than it is for men!

Women who have gone through the first two years of loss seem more open to the difficulties men face. However, all groups write that the greatest difficulties they believe—or think—men encounter are their inability to make a home, to nurture themselves, to be alone, and, interestingly enough, to have strong support systems made up of other men. "Men are more sought after, but I don't think they have male friends with whom to commiserate," says a women in the first year. More than one woman admits that men have many more members of the opposite gender who will help them, something most women do not have. "After all," a friend said to me recently, "how many men bring casseroles to women?" A casserole brigade might be nice; a home cooked meal from some man's kitchen would be a treat!

When a spouse dies, the remaining partner must take on many new responsibilities if she or he is able. Responders equate the problems of finances for women to those of homemaking for men. In the business world, there is a lot of financial and legal assistance available, and probably some already in place. Not so with home-making nor, as many women reported, with other aspects of choice, decision and activity that traditionally fall to the wife, even in today's more modern marriages and certainly in those of the older generation.

As the widow must find her own way, so must the widower. Usually he remarries. If he can cook and knows how to take care of himself and his home, he can continue independent of another marriage, should he wish to. "I've watched a couple of widowers through the years. These were capable men who could cook and do the taxes." This is from a woman in the first year group. She does not tell us whether they have found new marriages or relationships.

Not one person in the project has mentioned independence as something a man can grow into after his wife dies. Do we believe he's always had it? Of the sort we now cherish, the answer is probably "yes."

Of the sixty-five women who responded to this question, more than half wrote about the subject of men remarrying or finding a new relationship. The women who have remarried or are in positive relationships have returned to the paired world which, I believe, is where most of us would like to be again, could we find or be found by the "right man." Many of us have already admitted that it is difficult to contemplate surrendering our hard-won independence were we faced with the opportunity of marriage. One woman said, "Some widows have found new loves. I find this amazing, but it has seemed right for them. I can't conceive of exchanging my new closeness to my children, my step-children and grand-children for a new male friendship."

History, if we look deeply enough, tells us that widowhood was the only independent state for women in earlier, much more gender unequal societies. If there was inherited money or title, widowhood offered escape from what she had been as a wife. The idea for *The Merry Widow* did not spring fully developed from the forehead of Franz Lehar. Society allowed a widow much more freedom than a maiden or wife. If she had money, she had power, and she didn't have to do what she was told. In some civilizations, she could be a warrior.

Most women in the project seem to believe that marrying again is a necessity for a man, a constant fact as well as an open option. One woman said she believes men have a more difficult time reinventing themselves. Could it be that men reinvent themselves through another marriage? Does the need for nurture, a home, a caretaker, a cook and a warm bed loom so large that they eagerly move back into marriage? As one wag said, "Maybe they just can't learn to make decent coffee!"

The majority of responders do believe that men have at least as much or more difficulty dealing with their grief than women— and they believe their grief is similar. As one woman wrote, "I think that the deeper levels of loneliness and sense of abandonment and of all of the sadness that happens are experienced by everyone, whether they are male or female." The initial loneliness, the dread, trauma and despair may be the same or perhaps even greater—how do we know? However, many women believe that men are not able to reach out. They also believe that society does not allow men to grieve beyond a few weeks' time, and that men may bury their grief rather than work through it. As women, we really don't know these things about men. The plethora of books currently describing women to men, men to women and both to each other delves more deeply into relationships in business and marriage than into the lives of widows and widowers. Probably that will come soon. Almost daily there are articles about mourning, grief and how to handle both. Even popular mystery writers now dare to concern themselves with bereavement and reinvention, at least from the male point of view. Film heroes and heroines with a little extra age and the experience of losing a loved one are becoming more popular, more interesting—a nod to the aging Baby Boomers and how they continue to affect today's attitudes. We're all learning. With this project, we may be doing pioneer work.

⁘ ⁘ ⁘ ⁘

When the project was in its early months, I spoke with a professor of humanities at a large state university. His wife had attended Smith College. He said he thought it would be a great idea to send our questionnaire to one hundred of his male graduates. Although this did not work out, I will always appreciate his interest and continue to hope that such a situation might develop.

Going over their responses makes me wonder if the women in the project, truly if all women in our situation, occasionally are judgmental about the men who, like ourselves, are survivors. Perhaps a moment of resentment or bitterness? Not only because society accepts these men so readily, but because these men seem to enjoy playing the field, which is us, and, to stretch the metaphor, is ready for picking. Do these thoughts tempt us to argue that men are less sensitive to grief, less moved by death, less vulnerable? Not when we think seriously. We may wish that cultures were more even handed, for us as well as for women everywhere. We know we no longer have to be with a man to feel validated as a woman. Should we ask if the same idea with proper reversals holds true for men? Perhaps it does, perhaps not.

⁘ ⁘ ⁘ ⁘

A few years ago I discussed the project with two friends who are widowers. One is a more recent acquaintance, the other Jerry and I knew when his wife was alive and we were all involved in church work. As a result of our discussion, these men offered to take a look at what we were doing. Surprisingly, both worked through the entire questionnaire, although I expected them to answer only the questions we are dealing with in this chapter.

Claiming to be compulsive, one friend said he wrote for hours. The other, much more reserved, wrote simple, direct answers. Each man was deeply involved in his wife's illness. Both women died of cancer, prolonged deaths with, as I gather from their answers and understand from our conversations, moments of great hope between times of great sadness and despair. Many of the men's responses are remarkably similar to responses from women.

To the question about memorial services, one wrote that he found the service helpful because of the presence of many friends; the other said the service was positive, final and helped sum things up. As for the grief process, one man did not respond, but in conversation admitted he realized a year later that he had been experiencing grief all that time. The other found the many things that needed to be done almost overwhelming. He spoke of a sequence described to him by a priest: one week for mourning and then back to work; then one month and back to the social life; then one year and it's all over. He said he found that a wise statement. There was, at times, he said, increased depression "but nothing debilitating." And there was, early on, a moment of panic soothed by his son who came to his rescue at two-thirty in the morning.

Cards and letters were a great help. Families were the main stays for both men. Invitations to lunch, travel and theater—"even ones I could not accept"—assured the first man that he was still a member of society. He joined an adventurous hiking group. The exercise was good for him, he wrote, and he was forced to make new friends.

Neither man joined singles groups or grief therapy sessions. One added that he and his wife had not sought counseling with anyone except family, friends and a priest. Sharing memories was very important to both men. "I worry sometimes that people feel I am holding on to her memory too much. I honestly don't know, but I feel I do not want to dismiss her memory. She was too much a part of my life. I often wonder how couples who have married a second time are able to blend their old memories with their new memories. I still wear my wedding ring. I suspect it is a form of protection from marauding females. A dear friend publicly stated that I would remarry immediately since I wouldn't be able to live alone. She was wrong."

Helping other widowers? A card, a phone call, an invitation—always a visit. Neither man spoke of any particular advice.

The question of barriers among friends was difficult to transpose. The first man omitted a response. The second said his son gave him a long lecture on how he should treat women and how he should "watch out!" He admits that some aggressive women startled him. He did not see them again. Male friendships "were more difficult, since there is always the suspicion of homosexuality. The double standard: it's okay for women to be together, but not for men." He adds that he was never aware of any husbands being suspicious of his friendship with their wives. When one husband seemed uncomfortable, my friend ended contact immediately.

Anger? One man admitted to mild anger at her doctor on the initial diagnosis and at her for not discovering—or for ignoring—what was obvious. He said he blamed himself for what he called "various negligences." About anger, the second man said there was none. "I was too busy for anger."

In social situations, the first man wrote that a single male may go almost anywhere without embarrassment. But early invitations with small groups seemed a bit awkward, "especially if a new single female was specifically included." The other's response mentioned the fifth wheel feeling in social situations during the first year. He said he would ask to join people, to drive with them but he would not cling to a certain group. He entertained often, had no idea how society looked at him. At the time of his responding, he said he finds his social circle getting smaller. He no longer is invited to couples parties, regretfully, and now he would have no problem with a hostess pairing him with a woman.

Neither man had difficulty describing himself in regard to present retirement or past profession. Neither would offer information about marital status or problems unless asked directly.

About health, one man said he had an ulcer in the second year. The other realized early on that he would have to take care of himself. "Physical health was good in many ways," he wrote. Actually, he admitted he felt physically relieved because now he was responsible only for himself. "Frankly, it was a new and welcome experience." He added, "I refuse to let health hold me hostage."

About financial matters, both had planned well. One man's wife had handled their finances and financial planning, turning it over to him when she became too ill to continue.

Major difficulties? Dealing with household help and obtaining enough death certificates for the many, many requirements of bureaucratic procedures.

Finding a new balance? (We call this "Reinvention" and "Reinvention of Self" in the next chapter.) "Gradual but I knew for some years I would have to do it." "The turning point was between six months and the first year. I realized I could not wait for other people to provide me entertainment. If I was terribly lonely, there was always the phone, and I have lots of friends around the country. Most people are delighted to hear from you."

The more voluble of the two writes that now what he enjoys most as a widower and a single person is his sense of independence. And he enjoys getting things done. He is always busy.

Both men stay in close touch with their former professions, both like to travel. They enjoy opera and theater, attend often, usually with one of many female friends or with groups that include married couples. Even numbers seem important to them.

Social difficulties: "Being with female friends without giving the impression that I am looking for a permanent relationship," according to one man. The other believes friends sometimes hesitate to invite him because he is single, has no steady date, so they don't know whom to match him with. He says that now his friends fail to realize he is always ready to meet new people "and I think I can give a new date a pleasant evening, and we don't have to end up in bed with each other." His lonely times come in the evening and at night in an empty bed when the familiar presence and touch of his wife are no longer there.

Advice to someone faced with the recent or imminent death of his wife: "Keep working, keep up physical exercise, don't reject new friends." "When you know death is coming, make sure that all things have been discussed and discovered if not discussed. Make sure that all the family has had a chance to say goodbye. Make sure you have activities planned to keep you busy after the death. Don't sit around and be numb. I suspect some people feel that immediate activity lacks reverence and grief. To hell with that. You know how much you loved each other. Life must continue to be lived, and your spouse should be the first person to have said that.

"Contemplating a second marriage is difficult and probably should be put off for a year. Then anything goes. But don't do it just because you are lonely."

On the subject of how men and women grieve: "The similarities are emotional. The differences are financial, including experience in the world outside the home." "I haven't talked with other widowers about their feelings so I don't know. I do feel that widowers tend to shy away from each other. Perhaps because they don't want to waste time when they could be meeting women."

Both men are fine cooks. They entertain well, one often, the other occasionally. At the time of their writing, one had been a widower for six years, the other for three. Neither says he is looking for a second spouse. One told me he always knew he would be living alone in his later years. The other spends a lot of time telling people he will never remarry. And probably he won't. Both attend their churches quite regularly. Both are retired but still very active in many aspects of their professions. Their houses are well cared for, although they admit that finding the right help was a problem at first. One man has houses in two communities—the long time family home and a newer home he and his wife chose together. The other kept the lovely home he and his wife designed, but now is considering a move to a smaller place, probably a retirement situation. Both men remain deeply devoted to their families and their friends.

Earlier, I mentioned that I had been involved with my national church, on the board of the Presiding Bishop's Fund for World Relief (now Episcopal Relief and Development) that meets in New York City, and the College of Preachers at the site of the National Cathedral in Washington D.C. A few years ago, I was at an October meeting at the college. Over breakfast, I spoke with a priest who had just completed a book about his experience as a widower, his regeneration and his hope for the future. Across from us sat a man who, hearing our conversation, told us of his wonderful second marriage following his first loss. He said he had thought he could never be happy again, then discovered with his new wife a happiness greater than any he could have imagined. My friend and I were too deeply into our own discussion of sorrow and search to hear more of his story. I wish we had listened longer.

8

⁀ Reinvention ⁀

How long does it take to heal the open wounds of widowhood? How long does it take to accept what seem to be the limitations of your life? How long to recognize the abundant grace that you will encounter? How long to discover who you must become; to realize you are self-sufficient and independent; to understand the comfort of memories; to build on what has been; to make changes for your own sake; to find joy in what you are doing? When are you ready to risk moving on?

I'm reminded of the time, rate and distance problems we worked in elementary math. Is time the operative element? Time, healing time, will differ for each of us but it figures in the equation of where we are going and how we get ourselves there. We each have our own equation; we each are responsible for its solution.

Three years after Jerry McNally died, I had occasion to travel back to New York City where, in addition to attending a board meeting, I made time to lunch with the grand old lawyer who had guided us through our early business years. "How long has Jerry been gone?" he asked. I told him. "Three years," he said, " that's been enough time for grieving. Put this behind you, move on." No one had ever spoken to me like that.

Tempted to remind this man that he and his wife were still together, I ached to ask him why he dismissed Jerry's death and my grief so casually. I did neither. Later, I decided these hard words were a stern, caring mini-lecture about the way things ought to be. Lawyer-like, he had cut to the quick. It was time to take the harder way, to be, in contemporary lingo, pro-active about my future. I thought I had been doing very well. He made me realize there was still more to be done: more changes to be recognized and accepted as part of my growing. Although I could not dismiss what I felt for what had been, I had to recognize that, like everyone else, I was and would continue to be in a state of "becoming." Nothing could be static. Particularly my life.

⤳ ⤳ ⤺ ⤺

The three-year time frame is usually the accepted one. Some need more, some less, but by three years most of us have moved into or are ready for a new place in our lives. Has there been a turning point, a watershed, a series of epiphanies, a situation where we realized we could succeed in making a new life and feel good about it? These are the first questions we asked in this topic of Reinvention. Originally the topic was called "Reinvention of Self," as Barbara used it in her reunion report. Now I believe there is much more to reinvent than your self and, arbitrarily, I have made this change. We asked which aspects of your growth give you the most satisfaction? When did you begin to find satisfaction in your ability to accomplish things yourself, on your own terms, and to enjoy doing it? We also wanted to know what difficulties you still encounter and when you are most apt to feel lonely.

⤳ ⤳ ⤺ ⤺

Helen's Story (First year, continued)
"Reaching a true turning point may not be part of my life just yet. However, having a summer home which needs much time and

work gave me something challenging and creative to focus upon, and a sense of something that is mine in concrete terms. I continue to remind myself that I must survive. I have a responsibility to myself and a responsibility to our children to pave a road to healing and recovery. Having been widowed only three and a half months, that road ahead is long, wide and unknown. And yet, I already have moments when I find amazement in the strengths I've uncovered and skills surfacing that have helped me accomplish so much in a short period of time. My discovery that one has really to like one's self to survive the loneliness has become a rule to live by; anything less could be suicidal. The art of becoming independent and addressing accountants, bankers and other professionals has helped my self-esteem.

"Currently, my greatest difficulty is not having that special person on hand to talk things over with spontaneously or to give me a helping hand with items to be moved—a teammate, someone who already knows my ways, style and weaknesses. The moments of emptiness can be frequent on weekends. The eleven at night to three in the morning time period has become problematic, and new feelings are surfacing in missing that special time of comfort after an arduous day to settle in together and forget the day's woes."

➷ ➷ ➷ ➷

Our responders in the first year group agree that they are not there yet. And, of course, they aren't. However, they are moving ahead by making new friends, developing new interests, meeting challenges, traveling, and by taking time to think deeply about themselves and their futures. "I am really not there yet," wrote one woman, "although I have made plans to return to college next year to get an associate degree in a medical field which interests me and is opening up." Another woman said she thought having her own business helped, as did close family relationships. A plus for her was "having always been fairly independent." Two responses are particularly poignant:

"'Reinvention of self, even if not new, it is a wonderful phrase, one I have used often in the past months. Very helpful to all widows and a widower I used it on. I don't think I ever realized I couldn't, just knew I would have to, and will have to develop some kind of new life. At the moment, I still don't know what or possibly where it might be." "I am just now starting to think about a new life. I feel there is a need to keep a perspective of the old life sharing time with the new. Hopefully, the new things I've chosen to be involved in will be positive forces in the years ahead. But I must also keep some of the old ways as a reminder of so much good in my life."

Jane's Story (First year, continued)

"Following the memorial service, I escaped loneliness by traveling to Alaska, Cincinnati and to Aix en Provence, France, to visit our children and their friends. I made all of my own travel arrangements, drove myself to the airport in two instances. Had a great time and felt good about making my own way without an escort or tour group. I'm pleased to be getting on with my own life with purpose, planning ahead, doing things I enjoy, helping others, traveling. The challenge? I bought a new car by myself. Sold my old one, got an AAA printout of dealer costs, made an offer which was readily accepted. When I first went to the dealer, he asked me how I liked the color of the car. The difficulties? Dealing with the volume of mail from people whose lives were touched by my husband. And with their testimonials about his effect on their lives. I'm lonely when I come back to our home and find everything in order and empty. Once I strew a few things around, I feel a little more at home. I keep spilling tears when I write my thank you notes. I have a hard time with these."

Caroline's Story (First year, continued)

"Shirley: I hope your project goes along well. It's a wonderful way to help people in their grieving process to know they are not alone. I, myself, will have to see what comes next. I'm relishing having a lot of time and don't feel I have to rush out and accomplish something. The summer is filled with children's visits, the cottage and golf. When fall comes, maybe all the extra time and loneliness will loom too large. Who knows? I'm not rushing to plan anything at the moment. I retired from my part-time job after fourteen years just when David died. Still to early to see what my new life will be."

～ ～ ～ ～

Although most women in the second year group report that they also are in process, some say they have been helped by new responsibilities either in their chosen or in new fields or professions. One, who said she read books about widows and found them helpful, added, "The stiff upper lip approach was no help. I had to learn by doing it—that I could acknowledge and express despair and agony and live through it and come out the other side, and then begin to move off dead center. Filling out this questionnaire has been a useful process for me." "Still in transit from being his wife to being myself, with my work, my interests, my life" says another woman.

～ ～ ～ ～

Pat's Story (Second year, continued)

"About ten months after Peter's death, I was offered the directorship of the local literary council. I had always considered myself a strong back-up person but not necessarily a prime mover. With some trepidation, I accepted the job and found enormous satisfaction in this new and unexpected role. At this point—twenty months of being single—my work is my life. I have to work hard making myself develop more social outlets. When I'm working, I'm happy. When I'm not, I'm achingly alone, still. I find great satisfaction in what I have accomplished in my work. I have received professional recognition by my nomination to our statewide literacy professional board, and have given literacy workshops. For the first time in my working life, I feel truly professional. Putting so much effort into my work leaves little time for making social plans and contacts. I'm not happy being alone so much but I'm having trouble pushing myself."

Susan's Story (Second year, continued)

The turning point occurred in Susan's life, "when I became temporary, part-time assistant at a church other than my parish church where I had functioned almost exclusively for one and a half years after William died. This change for the better in my grief process was more a question of having my life-choice of the ministry affirmed than of curing my loneliness."

As for what now gives her great satisfaction, Susan says, " My ability to handle everything myself, from money to household maintenance. I own three houses. Also, my capacity for relating socially without a partner. I began to enjoy my new sense of selfhood once I got past the first anniversary of William's death. I am still basically lonely without a husband to share thoughts and feelings, to bounce ideas off of, to feel supported by in my various endeavors. I see now that William was really always the biggest fan of my rather unorthodox endeavors. Early mornings, before I can get out with people, are the loneliest times for me."

According to women in the three to five year group, turning points, moments of come-to-realize are difficult to determine. One woman said she is still in process, "I was numb the first year. I think I buried myself in work, working long hours. And then, the second year, I think I went a little crazy, did some traveling and felt I was beginning to wake up. Into the third year, I think the reality of missing him has moved in a much deeper way and I am only now coming to the recognition that I can redesign my life or reinvent myself." She added that people have told her she should start to remove the many, many pictures of her husband she has displayed in her home.

Other women say they, too, are still in process. Several indicate that there was a time when they began to feel better but they cannot pinpoint an event. A young mother, who has had to deal with more than one tragedy, does define a specific moment that occurred just a few months after her husband died. "Lying in the hospital after the birth and death of our son, I heard playing in my brain something I remembered from another time: 'You cannot control what happens to you, you can control how you react to it, how you deal with it, how you move on.' I knew I needed to dig down deep and find the strength to go on, to raise my sons, to find some joy again." Another response must be included because it recognizes that no matter how good a marriage was, some marriage habits and situations can be forgotten without bringing on any guilt. This is change as it should be. "My life improved quite quickly. Little things like not having to have football on TV, reading in bed as late as I want, not arguing about politics. But I miss having him to share three new grandchildren, putting on a wedding without him."

Some women shared stories of recognizing change as positive based on new self-confidence: "Shortly after his death, I took off and went to England with three female friends—two divorced and one widowed—whom I had known as tennis friends. I felt guilty that I enjoyed my trip so much. He had not wanted to go; I always had. He liked to go first class; we four went 'Bed & Breakfast.' I liked to spend less money so I could go more often!" "I was sheltered all my life from handling financial details. I paid monthly bills, but any undertaking—buying a car or house—was his forte. I realized I was on my own way to making a life for myself when I stood in the new townhouse I had purchased, with my own furniture and my own things. I know that he is proud of me." From a woman who had decided to remodel the family's lake house, "I changed the place that had been so dear to our hearts, and now I can enjoy being there so much more. Especially when I'm alone. It sounds trivial, but I had done something on my own, without his approval, and I guess I felt capable of making more decisions."

Jean's Story (Three to five years, continued)

"I really wasn't conscious of a watershed. I was always able to deal with the practical side of life by myself, and it was always a source of satisfaction to be able to do this. Truthfully, I always credited my Smith College experience for this. I continue to feel good about my ability to make a new life. Being able to deal with loneliness is a separate issue, and I expect this is something that will never change. My husband was my closest and best friend, and I will never cease to miss his companionship, his conversation and his sharing of the joys of family life. Both of our sons will be married this year, and it will be difficult for me not to think about how their father would have enjoyed these young women, and how they would have enjoyed him. His death meant I lost my best friend, confidant and companion. I feel most lonely when the occasions we expected to share occur, and I experience them alone. I also feel lonely when I see other people who still have this companionship, and it brings into sharp focus the fact that I no longer have it."

A friend of mine, a psychiatrist who is a widower, warned me that some women—and I suspect, some men—will put their lost spouse and lost marriage on a pedestal, often without fully realizing what they are doing. Although I see very little of this in the responses, I believe his warnings are important. He says it is better to accept the reality of that person and those years you were together. Nobody is perfect. No marriage is perfect, either. We all make mistakes; we all have character traits that are, at times, difficult to deal with. Relationships involve good times as well as bad. These are the realities of life. Because you cannot go back, dwelling on the past cannot make the present or the future any better. Reinventing the past is a bad idea. Use the past wisely, when you can, as you move through today to tomorrow.

⇒ ⇒ ⇐ ⇐

Several women shared their stories of new marriages and relationships: "Strangest of all, I have a happy companionship with a widower friend whom we had known for years. Neither of us ever dreamed of such a thing, but it has been a sort of delightful Indian Summer for us both." "I was fortunate to have fallen in love twice again—very healing—even though I also lost both of them, one to cancer." "Much as some of the articles had suggested would happen, I suddenly, quietly, felt I had rounded a corner after two years of widowhood and I became a sociable person again. In my third year, a wonderful widower, my husband's age and, in his gentle way like him, came into my life, almost like a reincarnation, and certainly a miracle, as I had never sought nor imagined a sequel to my already full life. It is as if I have been given a second chance to be to this person all that I failed to be to my first husband, and thus, literally, to be able to make a new life."

One woman wrote that she and her first husband had been estranged for several years. His illness had brought them back together, but the facts of the estrangement colored their last years as well as the early years of her widowhood. After his death, she wrote, "Some tried to assure me that I had been a good wife, that I was being too harsh on myself, but I alone knew of my impatience and lack of understanding, and that nothing anyone says can eradicate regret. I saw all my faults as a wife, and all his virtues that I failed to appreciate. I tried to say 'I'm sorry' during those last three sweet years, but for fear of crying, never said them. Had I been able to answer your questionnaire in the first two years of widowhood, I know it would have been a therapeutic experience. Even now, it has been helpful, five years after his death, and in a 'new life.' I made copies for my children, to leave them after my own death, so that they may be able to understand some things that have been hard for them to fathom."

A woman in the six to ten year group tells another story of new happiness in a new life, "There was a turning point for me two and a half years afterward, when I relinquished the thought that I needed to remarry. I was happy with my life, raising my children alone, etc. The same week that I truly let go of my former life and identity in this way, I flew to Florida to a meeting of a committee of a national board I was serving on. My current husband, whom I had known on this board, was there. We had known each other for one and a half years but never really talked. We fell in love that weekend. I am convinced that there was a God-given timing and link to the relinquishment and the second love."

⮑ ⮑ ⮐ ⮐

Ann's Story (Three to five years, continued)

"I do not see any turning point. At first, I had a sense of guilt about having no purpose in life. Before, I had a house to run for us as a couple. It felt sort of fruitless to run it for myself. Hence, the guilt. But I'm over that now. I have been very involved with three volunteer jobs, and I'm enjoying being of service in that way. In one of them, I have learned a lot. I have also become interested in town politics as they apply to one of my jobs. I feel good to be able to run my life and to be of some service to my community. I never had time for much volunteering, as I was working full time the last ten years before retirement. I also now enjoy having time to cultivate women friends. This has come on gradually. There are times when I have to take myself in hand and plan some activity outside of my house and grounds. Evenings are sometimes lonely, but sometimes I save chores to do then. I watch public TV some, but am not tied to it. Mostly, I prefer to read."

≈ ≈ ≈ ≈

Katherine's Story (Three to five years, continued)
"The clear watershed was my 40th Smith reunion. It was two years after Ed's death. Obviously, I felt good enough to go, and in the year after my illness, I had begun to reach out to people more than at any time in the past, so attendance was in order. Of course, I was dramatically slim. There are some good after-affects of illness."

Of her satisfaction and enjoyment in her growth, Katherine says, "I am simply friendlier and more conscious of other people. I had already been accomplishing things by myself but I do enjoy looking after my finances now, even though I don't do it very well. And I'm proud of the major renovations I made on the house, especially making an income apartment, which I did a year after Ed died. I'm still uncomfortable in larger groups when I don't know most of the people, especially since I no longer have that comfortable professional identity. Like Barbara Mulhern, I'm often alone but never lonely. But sometimes I do get tired of doing things by myself."

≈ ≈ ≈ ≈

Karen's Story (Three to five years, continued)
"Two years after Richard died, I went on a tour to New Zealand and Australia with a younger friend and was amazed at how much I enjoyed it. For the first time, I realized I could make friends on my own, come up with good decisions, travel and have fun. Although I will never stop missing my husband, I discovered single women can have fun, and I also found it possible and easy to relate to men on a platonic basis and enjoy their company. I'm pleased I am regaining self-confidence and the feeling of independence. I hope I'm no longer just a 'taker' but a 'giver' as well. I think you need self-confidence to be able to help others, and that's the most rewarding

thing for me. It took about two and a half years of 'singlehood' for me to get to that. However, I'm still struggling with unwanted investment and business matters. Loneliness strikes mostly when things go wrong, and I miss his good judgment and advice. No longer being needed is hardest, after really feeling vital to someone's well being."

⮫ ⮫ ⮪ ⮪

A woman in the three to five year group whose sharing has been strong and thought provoking writes, "If I have grown, it is in the areas of understanding of and forbearance for others. If your question asking when I began to find satisfaction in being able to do things on my own terms implies some sort of constraint on the part of living with one's spouse, I would say that there are always constraints to accomplishing things one's self. Loss of one's husband and the state of singleness are two in a long line, and if one hasn't learned to be one's self long before widowhood, it must be a terribly devastating experience."

During marriage, the relationship we have established with our husband has many specific boundaries, traditions and patterns. In most cases, these are positive, agreed upon mutually, and they are what make the marriage work. To find ourselves out of that relationship, even while we live in the same home, means that the boundaries, traditions and patterns have changed and will continue to change: new events occur, new problems arise, new opportunities come our way. We will have new choices and we will make them by ourselves.

The boundaries we enjoyed during our marriage will have to be replaced by others. This time, they will be largely of our own making as we react to the new circumstances in our lives. Unless we have mistakenly put our marriage and our husband up on that pedestal and intend to guard them forever, we do no harm to either when we find we are able to be different and to act differently than before. We are growing. We are becoming new.

On a day when a friend and I were speaking of another friend, we agreed that she had grown far beyond what we might have expected when we knew her as half of a married couple where the husband was very strong. She carried with her all the wisdom she gleaned from her long, successful marriage to a remarkable man. I have always believed that no experience is ever lost: the scars on our knees from roller-skating are still with us. The time two people spend in a marriage will affect each of them deeply. When one dies, we can assume that his or her influence—or some part of it—will remain with the survivor. We build on what has made us who we are over the years and use it to help us move beyond, sometimes far beyond, where we have been. And we must believe that this is what our husbands would want us to do.

⇒ ⇒ ⇐ ⇐

Two women in the six to ten year group spoke of new relationships that ended unhappily: "I thought I had my life together, or on the way to together again when, three and a half years later, I fell in love with an old friend whose wife had left him. However, it proved incredibly difficult to resolve, and I felt quite paralyzed by the whole incredible—to me—situation." "There were two turning points. The first was the first sexual adventure, a necessary liberation. The second was after a serious love affair that ended in betrayal and rejection. I had to fight my way back, rediscover the true sources of my strengths and weaknesses, accept being alone and accept being lonely. Something else will happen. I always knew I could make a new life. My husband knew that, too. I seem still to be discovering what the conditions of this life might be. Change is one of the constants. Change and discovery."

Others also speak of change and discovery, of growing when they were able to move away from their daily routines or, as one woman described it, "from the patterns of my married life." "After almost four years, I took a trip back to the place where our children were born and we had many friends. Although it was difficult to plan the trip, I realized during it and after I got home that I was finally healed, that I was a whole person who would always miss him but was ready and eager to get on with her life. In retrospect, I am amazed that it took four years." Another woman points to several important steps toward independence and self-sufficiency, through change. "When all the pieces finally came together—self-confidence, feeling of worth, financial understanding, acceptance that I could not control everything, friendships—they allowed me to look far enough ahead to make one plan that I knew would take a minimum of several months to carry out. And I did it in spite of family objections. I bought a twenty-foot boat! I think at this time, which was almost six years after his death, that I stopped feeling so vulnerable and began to open up more to the outside world. The glass wall came down."

꒰ ꒰ ꒰ ꒰

Betsy's Story (Six to ten years, continued)

After a year, I tried to make a new life by moving to a new job in another state. This was a mistake and a blessing. The job was a disaster, my ability to roll with it not too good, but I think it was something I had to do. It prepared me for really handling a great job back in my hometown. I learned I could be all right on my own. Accomplishing things on my own terms was a process through my marriage to Ted and it has continued. Began in second year with that good job, then I became involved with an Alcoholic Coalition in my church and served as president on its National Alcoholic and Drug Coalition. I have discovered new talents, made a whole new, extended family of friends. I have traveled to neat places and made a difference in a significant number of lives. As for difficulties, I have tended to have an underlying sadness and at times feel lonely. This happens most when I am overtired or stressed at work. It's sometimes hard not to have someone to come home to, to share the good and the bad. However, the longer I live alone, the more contented I am, and doubt if I'd marry again."

⇒ ⇒ ⇐ ⇐

Judith's Story (Six to ten years, continued)

"After about three years, I decided to find other volunteer work. I had been in an elementary school library. I learned braille so I could transcribe children's books for the American Brotherhood for the Blind. Since I learned that language, I am almost never lonely and can lose myself in a book as I pound away on my brailler. Also, I became involved in the local library and the board of the Community Center. I decided to buy a new car six years after Gene's death and was very apprehensive but found I could do it and not be put down by the salesman. Since then, I decided to sell my house, which was really too big for one person, and move into a retirement facility with Life Care. I am quite satisfied with that change, and I enjoy where I am now."

⇒ ⇒ ⇐ ⇐

Beverly's Story (Six to ten years, continued)

"I knew all along I could make a new life. I just had to do all I could for him and handle all the practical demands before I had the luxury of time for me. I knew I'd have the rest of my life to concentrate on me, once he was gone. I was always able and happy to do things myself, but I am lonely when I do not have a partner—a date—at parties and other couple activities."

⇒ ⇒ ⇐ ⇐

In the more than ten year group, women reported that work was the basis of a turning point, as was traveling, moving to a new place, experiencing a sudden beauty and peace, and finding new, happy relationships.

⇒ ⇒ ⇐ ⇐

Stephanie's Story (More than ten years, continued)

"There really was no watershed. It happened slowly, the process is not completed. I doubt it ever will be. After each accomplishment I feel good, and the boost pushes me a little farther. But I will always wish my husband knew about the things I have managed. The biggest hurdle was surviving the death of our youngest daughter from leukemia and then picking up my life again. Recognition of my own capabilities came slowly. I am still hesitant to 'adventure' into new activities. I don't go exploring in out lying areas. I'm more comfortable in my own neighborhood but when I push myself beyond my boundaries, I feel the glow of accomplishment. There are still hurts when I feel slighted."

Connie's Story (More than ten years, continued)

"I decided to leave the big city. Life was very simple for me there. I really missed the Orient where we had spent so many years. Santa Fe—for those who know it, 'another foreign country'—was the solution. I knew I would make new friends. I would have to make an effort, something I did not have to do in that big city home. I felt I had to start living in a new place. Frankly, I have always been able to accomplish things that interest me, such as serving on several boards. I don't believe that has changed, except for the two-year period after Steve died when I was a mess. I worry a little bit about the future. Two of my friends tell me they don't like my driving. I don't believe I do feel lonely but I treasure my moments alone. I worry about things: do I have major medical coverage? I belong to the Hemlock Society, which is a comfort."

As I said earlier, my friend Connie and I traveled together. During her happy life in Santa Fe, she made many, many good friends, joined many important causes. One day I heard that Connie was over in Vietnam, traveling up rivers in a very small boat, stopping at small villages, working to educate the people to preserve their beautiful cranes, not eat them. She returned safely. A few years ago, she was killed when a tree, gnawed by a beaver, fell on her as she and her family were canoeing near the shoreline of the lake she loved so much.

⤙ ⤙ ⤚ ⤚

I believe that for as long as we live, we are never finished. Our processing is never complete, life goes on, change persists. What we must do is work with what we have in our past, our everyday lives and in our visions. And we work to move the three closer together. There are times when we are interrupted by life's surprises, some of them good, some not. In this project, we have been looking at a particular time in our lives. We wish it did not exist, but it does. It has changed us, forced us to learn about ourselves in a new context. Even the strongest admit that this is difficult.

Difficult, too, is the loneliness. We get used to it, we think about it less and less, but it's there, waiting for us. I must assume that remarriage solves many of the problems of loneliness. For the rest of us, they still come and go, sometimes unexpectedly. Several say there are advantages to living alone, but I do not believe they ameliorate all lonely feelings. We can be lonely in a crowd. We can be lonely for many different things. Here is how one woman in the six to ten year group dealt with her life and her loneliness, "For me, moving into a new and smaller place to live was more than an 'outer' turning point. I'm a nest builder. This was, in a way, my first home alone. I spent five years there, and it was a mixture of comfort and struggles. I kept on simplifying my methods, letting go of so many things I'd had—or thought I had—to carry on for others. I sorted mentally through successes and failures, recognized what my assets as a person were, looked at what I could improve on, made a partner of loneliness by christening it 'solitude to grow.' It was a re-charging time that pushed me forward to try new things."

⤙ ⤙ ⤚ ⤚

As to the way women tell us where and how they find themselves in the process of moving ahead, three things stand out in the responses. One: women are glad, and sometimes astonished, that they have made progress in handling the two aspects of single responsibility they most dislike: things financial and mechanical that involve automobiles and household tasks classically in the male domain. Two: of course, women deeply miss the companionship of their husbands. The wish for this companionship is widow-generic. Other kinds of companionship will bring fulfillment, but you must be open to them and you must pursue them. Three: accounts of growth, satisfaction in achievement and enjoyment of both that are positive far outnumber any that are negative. We survive by moving ahead, with courage and, hopefully, humor, and by developing or finding again the self-confidence that enables us to continue. It can be done, and women are doing it!

In response to our question about growth, several women shared interesting ideas. From women in the first year group: "If you consider it growth to enjoy things, I guess I started to enjoy some things once again after a few months, especially music, dance and art museums. I can't say I find any satisfaction in an ability to accomplish things myself in the two areas of my greatest lack of expertise: finance and the mechanical. Maybe time will give me a more accepting attitude here, but I do wonder. I still regard these areas as nuisances, or worse, impositions. But I do detect progress in the financial area." "I find satisfaction in little things: reading directions, assembling equipment, figuring out the computer, refinishing furniture." "Settling my husband's estate solo was a source of enormous satisfaction. I had always been a doer so making decisions came easily to me. I am poor, no, really terrible at fixing things around the house. My husband was a past master at this, so I am learning how to bang a nail or swish a paint brush about forty-three years too late." "I get some satisfaction out of managing my home and my finances, both of which I never had done before." "Overcoming the devastation and regaining my sense of independence has been a slow but steady progress. Since I had long been accustomed to self-accomplishment, it has been reassuring to find it again, after a long period of depression and sloth. However, I do find I take great care to involve myself in the activities, both professional and personal, that bring me the most satisfaction."

Most women in the second year group have made great progress: "Went through the motions successfully, but only in the past few months really began to feel totally myself and proud of it. Love job, built bookshelves in my home, made changes, plan to travel." "Being able to handle administrative details of the estate, take care of taxes, all household decisions and expenses, and to learn to believe that I could manage it all well enough. This has helped me feel much more competent and independent than before."

One response in the second group shares a different idea, "It is probably good that I have outlived my husband. He was not as self-sufficient as I in some things. But how grand it would have been to have had twenty more good years together." Almost all of us can say "Amen" to that last sentence. About the first, I think many of us believe we are better survivors than our husbands might have been. We are the nurturers, we have the ability and skills to make many friends, we can run a home, and we know how to network beyond the business world. I wonder if the Baby Boomer generation will tip the scales in the other direction, even slightly, leaving more widowers as time progresses. Some members of this group are already in our project. Would they agree that they and their peers have achieved more equality between the work and attributes of men and women, in home and business, than members of their parents' generation? Do they wonder what will happen in their adult children's generation?

One woman from the Boomer group tells us that now, when new trouble comes, she knows "this is not by any means the worst thing that has happened to me." This same woman has made a new life of which she is and should be very proud. "The fact is that I have been able to pull all the pieces together and build a new life for the three of us which does include some fun and some quality." From another woman who has made remarkable progress, "My professional growth is extremely satisfying: to know that I have begun a new career and founded my own business, which is successful, feels great. I am also extremely pleased with the growth and development of my children. They are three neat, successful children whose scars don't hamper them, and I take great pride in having successfully raised them. Personally, I feel good about all aspects of my growth. I realize I have not only survived one of life's most devastating experiences but I am a better person for it."

A third writer tells of a different reality during the first years following her husband's death. He was 36. "Loneliness, wanting to have more male companionship, lack of a sexual relationship, energy consumed by my small children, having to live on a tight budget, 'short fuse,' sometimes." However, after four years of raising her young children alone and of growing during that time, she wrote that she was married again, happily, to another wonderful man. She added she is working on a grief recovery program for her church. Her husband is deeply involved. She says, "There is a need for male leadership as well. This is not just women's work!" Beyond grief counseling, there really is a role for men to play. Many find it in platonic acts of friendship, concern and caring. A husband or a single man in his role as a co-worker may suggest lunch so you and he can discuss important professional decisions that affect both of you. There are husbands who will help you hang Christmas lights or cut dead branches off a tree; men who are gracious and caring because they can't be any other way. You know them already; you may be fortunate enough to meet others under new circumstances.

⌒ ⌒ ⌒ ⌒

My second travel experience, a year and a half after Jerry died, was with a Smith College Walking Tour in Ireland. (The cover photo was taken on that trip.) The group was made up of four couples and a number of single women, most of them widows traveling two by two. This is when I traveled with Connie, having met her earlier through mutual friends. How often I wish I had known her years before. Of the four couples, one stayed together, walked together, sat and ate together. They were friendly and gracious when group projects required their presence but, for the most part, it was obvious they preferred to be alone. The other three husbands and wives mingled constantly and separately with each of us. During meals they chose to join various groups, often the husband at one table, the wife at another. The men helped everyone across the high styles and slippery rocks. Their sharing made the tour even more pleasant. They were outstandingly thoughtful people, secure in their own relationships, able to enjoy each person as much as we enjoyed them.

A few years later, when a Smith College tour group came to Santa Fe, I recognized one of the women as an Ireland walker. She told me that her husband had died two years earlier. I was glad to remind her of our happy trip together, of his charming involvement with us, and of their kindness. I am sure our taking time to speak further about him, and about our own situations, made the visit more meaningful for her in a special way, as it did for me.

⤳ ⤳ ⤳ ⤳

On the subjects of relationships with men such as dating and marriage, some responders say they would like the opportunity to meet compatible men. Several, as you already know, have found great happiness in second or third marriages, others mentioned finding satisfactory companionship. After all, it is the husband who is gone, not the libido. While we did not dwell on these subjects in the project, we did discuss them among ourselves. One of us found a good relationship with an old friend to be, for a time, very rewarding and a lot of fun. All three of us have friendships with men, but not necessarily in a steady dating or companion sense. I suspect that every widowed woman, from time to time, thinks about the possibility of another marriage regardless of its probability. I would have to be deeply in love before I considered another alliance. Reluctance to give up the independent life-style I have achieved may make me unmarriageable. My age is a great factor as is the fact that the idea of a new life with a new man scares me. Am I still in love with Jerry? I have found no one to take his place. If there were to be a new husband, I would have to help him make his own place, not take Jerry's.

Women who marry again move back into the couples' world, into what we may still see as the cultural norm. It is good news that a friend has found happiness in a second marriage. If we are honest, it is also quite natural for us to feel a twinge of jealousy as we rejoice with the new couple. But remarriage will not happen for most widows. After a certain age, many women become wary of a second marriage when "wife" will so quickly become "caretaker." If the love is deep enough, that may work. We hope that love, not need or desperation, is the operative word in every new alliance. Perhaps those of us who say "not for me" would change our minds—and hearts—if faced with the opportunity of a true and fully reciprocated love. Who can tell? Many admit they would not give up their present independence, they enjoy it too much. Dates, escorts, companions, close friends—these are what women say they look for and wish for. If a man and woman—and how often it is the remaining two of a happy foursome—fall in love, marriage or a committed relationship may be ideal for them, families and finances permitting. As a woman in the six to ten year group reported, "I am content, having filled the void that was greatest for me." She adds, "It was, however, very difficult for me in some ways to leave our town, my friends and commitments, and begin anew. I mourn that life in some ways."

In the context of reinvention, many women comment that, despite all their progress, loneliness is still a problem, loneliness and lack of a partner. As we said earlier, most of us agree that women do not need to be defined by a relationship with a man—a good thing for many of us since available men are in such a minority. What about men? Does the fact that widowers usually remarry make it easy to assume that men need this proof of who they are, this affirmation of their sexuality, in addition to the caring and companionship marriage brings? Can men compartmentalize their grief? The thought does occur. Is it a criticism? I'm not sure. There is a completeness to marriage. Women understand this. So do men.

≈ ≈ ≈ ≈

When I was a youngster, my favorite series of books were L. Frank Baum's Oz stories, later continued by his daughter. One book, I believe it was *The Patchwork Girl of Oz*, told about a creature made of patchwork by a magician's wife. The wife asked him to bring the girl to life as her servant. The wife would use her when there was work to be done. Then the wife would put the girl away in a corner until another day when more work was needed. The story did not turn out as planned; the patchwork girl received more brains and a different character. Thereby hangs the tale. I have often thought the wife had a good idea, with a few broader applications.

A year ago, I met a woman who had solved her escort problem. She had a dear friend, a man who was, as she said "always available" in a situation they both enjoyed. "We go out together, no strings attached, a permanent friendship. We call each other when we have something to do." I understand that many women have friends with whom they travel, male friends, in platonic relationships. I wonder about the permanence of these arrangements. Perhaps that is not important. I traveled to New York City with a friend, a widower, and two married couples, long time friends of his when the six of them

were together. It was fun—good food, good theater, good people—
and there was the thrill of being back in that wonderful city. But I
was very lonely. Watching the subtle interaction of each married couple
made me sad and very much aware of my own losses.

⁂

"Reinvention of Self," as listed in the questionnaire, includes
questions about how women handled their recurring difficulties with
loneliness. We miss the man. We miss the marriage. We are in a
different place but we have brought these truths with us. We need to
discover new meanings for the words we use to describe our feelings.
Despite our dictionaries, I believe each of us has her own definitions
for words such as lonely, loneliness, lonesome, single, alone and
solitude. Were you to ask five friends to define these words, at least
two or three will say they find positives in each, particularly as time
goes beyond the first or second year. A friend whose marriage was
not like yours—how many are?—will offer other shades of meaning.
Is it possible to solve the problems of loneliness? Not entirely. But
women are trying. Responses to the questionnaire viewed as soft
statistics gave us the opportunity to show what it is about their efforts
that might be helpful to others.

First year:
- I do something or go somewhere.
- I still have one cat and having someone/something in the house
  that needs and asks for attention keeps the place from being empty.
- I immediately get into some kind of home busy work and with
  the mind busy, it all falls into place, somehow.
- Music is a help, reading, VCR. If I feel particularly lonely, I will
  pick up the phone and call a long distance friend. That always
  works.
- (Two women have grandchildren living with them. They say that
  helps.)

- I find it difficult to handle exciting and beautiful experiences without longing to share them with him, although I do feel, after some nine months, this aspect of things is getting better.

Second year:
- I have a darling cat. That helps.
- I no longer feel lonely because, in these two years, I have become used to my aloneness and face it down with my love of life and my self-sufficiency.
- (Early morning difficulties diminish when she gets out with people.)
- I'm still struggling with being alone, but making progress.
- I'm often alone, but never lonely.

Three to five years:
- I plan something special with friends who share the same memories of Christmas, his birthday, our anniversary, etc.
- You do have to make an effort.
- Loneliness is not an every day problem for me now.
- Like Barbara Mulhern, I'm often alone, but never lonely.
- I am never lonely. If one is, they should call someone else who is alone, go to dinner, a movie, anything for enjoyment.

Six to ten years:
- Still occasionally lonely, but I think a lot of it is a natural human condition. I do something. I call a friend, I walk, I read. Dinner times can be rough.
- Loneliness is a sense of not being quite complete. I continue to learn to complete myself, not to be completed by another.
- My difficulties are minor and can no longer be tied to being alone. For myself, I am no longer lonely very often.
- I seldom feel lonely as all three of my children live close by. When I am alone, I enjoy it. I read, watch TV, do needlepoint, etc. Also, I have a dog.

- The longer I am alone, the more contented I am. I doubt if I'd marry again.
- Any difficulties I have now are of my own making. The best cure for loneliness is simple: just look for someone lonelier than you are. Reach out!

More than ten years:
- I fight loneliness with a vengeance and will not accept it. Reading, TV, friends, music and a wonderful pet are my answers.
- I am pretty independent now.
- Something will trigger a memory, but I try to savor it instead of dwelling on it. I have found that solitude is rejuvenating when it occasionally comes to me.
- I sometimes feel lonely with my friends who have husbands. However, I chose not to marry, twice.
- I'm not at all the same person I was. I have learned to fill most of those "empty times." I think of him often. I miss being married to him but I've accepted this as part of my life. I'm pleased with who I am and look forward to finding who I will become.

Recently, when Mary Wydman and I were having another discussion about our lives, we agreed that we have reached what we would call a good, normal place. We have close ties to our family members. We each have many friends with whom we spend a lot of time. Mary does this here in Santa Fe, in Cincinnati and several other places she often visits. My Santa Fe friends and I plan evenings together at least once a week. I have two friends with whom I speak almost every day. My friends and I have set up schedules that include weekly lunches and entertainment. We have season tickets to concerts and the Santa Fe Opera. We tutor in the public schools, we work on non-profit boards, we travel together—now not as much and not as far. When Mary and I are together, we share sadness and happiness, we discuss ideas that are serious, some that are silly. We have fun. As Mary says, "I like my life now. I am lonely, sometimes, but most of the time I'm happy." I agree. The solitude of my home appeals to me. I enjoy entertaining but am glad when the party is over. I love having guests but am glad when they leave. Sometimes I want to be alone. When I can, I do things according to my own schedule. My volunteer work keeps me involved, but sometimes I wonder whether life without that work's requirements might be even better. I have no intention of finding if this it true. I like being busy. I like charity planning: I am good at it. I am becoming more aware of the fact that my life experiences have brought me what may be a kind of wisdom. Often, I have an idea of what might happen next in a situation that is somewhat familiar, how it will turn out, how to handle the results. This is something I can share, something that makes me valuable to my communities. This is a "come to realize" part of my story that is very exciting.

≈ ≈ ≈ ≈

The final question about Reinvention asks what women would say to a friend whose husband is dying or has just died—a way to begin the process, to shed a little light on what might happen. If you are in the first year group, what can you say to a friend who is about to experience problems so close to your own? Were there things you wish had happened, or happened differently? Are there truisms you want to share? Will speaking of them be helpful to her? If she seems inclined to listen, go ahead. Some have said that unless you are asked, giving advice is a not a good idea. But how do these women know what to ask for?

Generally, women say the subject of finances is most important, albeit touchy and very personal. A common thread. If a wife has not already established a financial partnership with her husband, she is heading for trouble. She needs help. Before he is claimed by his illness, should she come to the bedside with a notebook and pencil, ready to take down information about bank accounts, investments, and insurance policies? The sad answer is yes. Financial questions are more than appropriate if he is able to respond. Does she know his lawyer, his accountant, his banker? Where are the files, where are the bankbooks, the stock records, the tax records? Where is the safety deposit box key? To ask and to discover are not bad manners, grasping or in poor taste. This is her business. This is her survival.

⌒ ⌒ ⌒ ⌒

Another common thread: take time to talk with each other. "I'll never regret having lived night and day in my husband's hospital room during the last month of his life. But we didn't say goodbye. Talk about death. Say goodbye." This advice comes from a woman in the first year. From one in the second year, "Take opportunities remaining to say the important things. Don't hide your emotions from your spouse."

Were these women able to talk with their husbands about death, about what was happening and going to happen? If they were, that's wonderful. If not, were they speaking from a wish list, hoping to help other women avoid what had become their own regrets?

My own reflections lead me to ask if you were not able to do these things, then what? Is it ever possible to have no regrets; to have accomplished all you wanted to do; to have said everything, done everything? No. Omissions you recall later may bring sadness, sometimes guilt, until you understand that it was important for you and your husband to do things in your own way. That's the only way you and he had.

A book on experiences of one woman's widowhood, published several years ago, began with a long account of the days the writer and her husband spent calmly talking about their past, their present, and their hopes for her future, her decisions and cares to come. Jerry's and my experience wasn't like that, couldn't have been. He had a Hickman implant that the hospice nurse and I attended to. It didn't lessen his need for the morphine that, while covering his pain, was also slowly stealing his mind. Then we learned that a spinal epidural, a new procedure, would make him less dependent on that difficult drug. It did, but necessitated five days in ICU, not a good experience. The implant gave us all more time, good time, to be together. I told him I would stay in our beautiful new home. Then, that last day, I told him he was dying. He said he knew it and was not afraid.

I never did finish that book, but what I read raised a few nagging questions that continued to surface for a year or two. Did we do enough? Was something seriously missing in the way we handled our final days together? Could we have managed to spend more time talking, planning, finalizing? Was their parting better than ours? I felt not, but how did Jerry feel? I'll never know.

≈ ≈ ≈ ≈

Will you accept the idea that dying is something each of us has to do alone, at least in a human sense? The moment must come when, in dying, we move beyond our surroundings into another space defined by whatever our faith is or is not. It is a time when nothing more can be done for us by our families, doctors, friends. Obviously it is a sudden time, when things must be left unsaid and undone. The trappings and attendants at a death, whether in hospital, at home or where an accident takes place, must cease to matter in a certain instant. My church prays for a peaceful death, more in a spiritual sense than a physical one, I believe. Death is beyond our control, beyond our knowledge, beyond us. Whatever we do for the dying person, if it is done with love, I believe it is enough. What more can we do? Do you think the dying person remembers everything? Does he carry all the memories of dying with him to wherever the next place is? I doubt it. For those left behind, the next thoughts must be about the living, and how you survive the inestimable loss.

Two weeks after Jerry died, the surgeon who had done the epidural implant came to our home to talk with us about his death. We had questions. His answers, a gracious gift to all of us, helped our understanding of what happened during those last hours. I hope other bereaved families have this same opportunity.

⌒ ⌒ ⌒ ⌒

Helen's Story (First year, continued)

From her perspective of four months, Helen says she would tell a newly widowed friend, "Life is going to be difficult for a while. Allow yourself to feel whatever feelings strike you. Expect to be struck with feelings and pain when you least expect them. Allow yourself the right to experience pain or joy. Find friends who allow you to express yourself without having to hide feelings. Avoid those who tell you how you should feel or who try to control your life more than you wish."

⌒ ⌒ ⌒ ⌒

Jane's Story (First year, continued)

"I tell them that it will be a hardship no matter whether it is an expected death or not. Unexpected death is devastating to deal with. In my case, I tell them I'm happy for John but sad for me. I am in tears as I write these lines."

⌒ ⌒ ⌒ ⌒

Caroline's Story (First year, continued)

"Try to understand your business/financial matters as thoroughly as possible. Actually do the work if possible, so you can know the questions and get answers. Keep strong contact with friends so you have people and activities to fill your life."

⌒ ⌒ ⌒ ⌒

Other women in the first year group offered these comments: "Live day to day." "Give yourself as much time as you can. Be good to yourself. Plan to get out of the house. Believe in yourself." "Avoid friends who tell you how you should feel." "Think of the good times you had." "Reach out and help others. Be patient with yourself and with others as they struggle with their grief and ways to relate to yours. Do not compare your grief to that of another." "Try to become a person in your own right, not just half of a team." "Accept all help, caring, invitations and activities that come your way. Try to return some of them. Don't try to be brave. Don't make any changes for a year." And, finally, "Since each person's grief-experience is unique, the best advice I can offer is the reassurance that the acute anguish does diminish and that life can again be fulfilling and enjoyable. This I really believe!"

≈ ≈ ≈ ≈

Pat's Story (Second year, continued)

"Learn to be accessible, to respond when people reach out, to accept help when offered, and to ask for it when it's needed."

≈ ≈ ≈ ≈

Susan's Story (Second year, continued)

"Assurance that the passage of time will lessen the pain; that some real good can come out of the radical life change; that it is possible to feel closer, in some ways, to your dead husband than ever before. He is always with you, and the two of you will be reunited."

≈ ≈ ≈ ≈

Other women in the second year would offer these thoughts to a friend whose husband is dying or has just died: "Think ahead about where and how you may want to live in the future. Get lots of help: people are wonderful." "Try to expand. Be aware that the loss will be devastating. Go through it, not around it."

Jean's Story (Three to five years, continued)

"Work! Having a significant activity or job or project is the only thing that fills the days with meaning. Your life cannot be dependent on someone else, because ultimately you are always alone."

❧ ❧ ❧ ❧

Ann's Story (Three to five years, continued)

"The thing I feel most strongly about is that women should know ALL about financial matters: where things are kept, what records to keep. And they should have plenty of experience with the checkbook. At one point, I kept the office checkbook and that of my mother. Too many women are left out of this type of activity, even educated women."

❧ ❧ ❧ ❧

Katherine's Story (Three to five years, continued)

"Hang in there! The grieving never really ends completely, but once the intense period is over, the independent life afterward can be a newly exciting period."

❧ ❧ ❧ ❧

Karen's Story (Three to five years, continued)

"Give yourself time to heal, certainly months, maybe years, if necessary. Being widowed is like having an amputation. A huge chunk of your life is gone forever. And there is no grafting or transplant available to replace the father of your children. Get you own credit cards before you need them, with your own number, not your husband's. It is still very difficult to convince businesses that we are financially reliable if we don't have jobs."

❧ ❧ ❧ ❧

Other women in the three to five year group also stress working, volunteering, keeping busy, reaching out: "If one of the few acquaintances I know who is newly widowed asks me, I am happy to give specific examples of what helped me in a very practical sense. This was going back to work." "Share your grief and help others by sharing theirs. Some friends will fade out, new friends will appear. Talk about it, don't do it alone. Develop a support group." " Know that loneliness strikes when least expected. Trust God and time to help since nothing else will. Learn independence. You will find a way. Look up, look out, look ahead! Exercise. Breathe deeply. Take time to grieve, or be angry, then believe that the good years live on, the bad ones fade, and there is a good menu of possibilities to choose from. Listen to what you feel and trust it and give yourself time."

Another woman writes, "Each experience of becoming widowed is unique in its circumstances. I would react accordingly by giving a friend lots of space and privacy if that seemed best, or being very attentive, supportive, a good listener, checking in regularly, getting her out of the house to do something pleasant. Whatever way, I would react, of course!"

I believe that the women in this three to five year group and in the later groups are offering suggestions from their own positive experiences and from what they now believe would have been more helpful than the help they did receive. Giving them that opportunity was the point of this question.

꩜ ꩜ ꩜ ꩜

Betsy's Story (Six to ten years, continued)

"I think being there and listening is the best way I can help. It's terribly painful, and I don't think you can avoid the grief. You must go through it. Gradually you can get on with life. It's been eight years for me. I can look back and see great personal and spiritual growth, many accomplishments, satisfactions—and fun."

꩜ ꩜ ꩜ ꩜

Judith's Story (Six to ten years, continued)

"My only advice would be to take one day at time, put one foot in front of the other and hope that God will help when one most needs help." Judith enclosed the familiar poem by Thomas Gray that includes these lines, "Be not like others, soon undone . . . For my sake turn again to life and smile . . ."

Beverly's Story (Six to ten years, continued)

"If it's imminent death, discuss everything you need to so you won't be left with emotional unfinished business. Do what you and your spouse feel is best. Don't worry about pleasing anyone else. It's your life, not theirs. If it is a recent death, I'd say take care of you. Do whatever it takes to help you heal."

Other comments from women in the six to ten year group continue to suggest what the future will hold and how to get to that future: "Don't rush into marriage. Don't mourn or be angry about losing old friends." "You're stronger than you think. Deal with your feelings, no matter what. Let your friends help you." "Tell your friends what you need if they ask." "Don't skip over anything. Don't pretend what is happening isn't happening. Do everything with love." This wonderful advice could be important for women either side of the death. Another woman offers advice that she believes is primary to healing, growth and reinvention. This is advice we have heard before, but it is well worth emphasizing. She says you should accept the early invitations to dinner, lunch or the movies—whatever comes along—as often as you can. And then you must begin to return those invitations, even if you have to force yourself to do so. As she says, "It gets easier once you make the first move!"

Stephanie's Story (More than ten years, continued)

"If you are not a native of your community but a transplant, as we were, develop a support system. Learn to ask for help so you will be comfortable with asking for help when your husband dies. Have interests. I went back to my interest in creative writing. It's given me a lot of satisfaction!"

≈ ≈ ≈ ≈

Connie's Story (More than ten years, continued)

"Let your friends help you. Hang on to them and tell yourself that anger, extra grief and self-blame are normal. Time, and only time, will help."

≈ ≈ ≈ ≈

"Get rid of his clothes ASAP!" says a thoughtful and practical woman. She is absolutely correct. The longer his clothes remain in the closet, the more difficult it will be to prevent them from becoming a strange memorial. Give them away quickly. Those beautiful sport coats can be enjoyed by someone else—his brothers, his sons. Or pack them up and take them to a charitable institution. If you are lucky, as one woman said, your children will help you do the job or they will do it for you.

≈ ≈ ≈ ≈

In another context, here is how one woman feels about helping a friend who is newly or about to be bereaved, "You really can't give advice, but you can share what worked for you. I think I would begin by asking her how she was feeling and encourage her to talk about it with me. You have to be careful to talk about feelings with the right people. This isn't everyone's cup of tea and can do more damage than good. It also depends on what's in her life after her husband dies. I would probably tell her to be very good to herself until a comfort level came to pass and I would let her know it takes generally two and a half to three and a half years, if she asked." This woman adds, "This is a tough question!" And it is. You notice that she begins by saying you cannot give advice. Another woman in this group agrees, "Advice? None! Sensitivity, response to signals, questions, sharing thoughts and reactions to similar situations, as much as is helpful and welcome. There's a lot of gratuitous advice giving in all of us and it's often best left unsaid." Advice that moves close to control is unwelcome and can be devastating. A good rule of thumb: give advice if you are asked. Another: always add that you are speaking from your own experience, which may well be different from hers.

This woman writes from her own difficult experience, "My strongest advice to widows who are also parents of young children is to avoid protecting them. Be open with them, willing to share grief, allowing them to express anger and sorrow. Be willing to seek professional help before it is too late, and willing to advocate for them even when so-called experts disagree. And for all widows with or without children, do for yourselves what you would wish your husbands would do for themselves had the situation been reversed."

Other women add these suggestions:

"Don't push for solutions. Death isn't a problem to be solved."

"Remember to laugh, often."

"I think my having been through it makes it easier for a new widow to communicate her suffering, and I find it very easy to remember mine."

"Know that you will grieve; be prepared for the gamut of emotions that will assail you. In time, you, too, will be whole."

"I would tell her what happened to me: how fragile I was, how I had to learn to make plans, to learn to be alone. And I would add that she, too, will learn these things. It will happen."

"I would listen, listen, listen. Sometime I would tell her that she will have to make an heroic effort to get started again—but I won't say that until she seems ready to hear it."

"When I look back I realize that I needed some praise, someone to tell me that things will get better. So now I find things I can compliment, and I try to be positive because I know it's the truth. Things will get better. She needs to hear that."

"Think of your newly-singled life as an opportunity to be the kind of woman your husband would be most proud of. Show your family the best of yourself!"

Finally, "Remember, you have been loved!"

Epilogue

We used the stories widows shared with us to develop a project that is more than refuge, it is reference—earnest and poignant. Perhaps it is a kind of curriculum. Certainly it is a series of life lessons presented to help others move beyond the tragedy that occurs when husbands die. Teaching survival skills by example, it urges widows to realize they can discover new lives for themselves, futures that are good, fulfilling and happy.

Mary Wydman wrote about the "new Me" it was her responsibility to become. In her coda, Barbara Mulhern spoke of the grief that has turned into gratitude for her husband and for the part her memories play in her present life. "Get on with it" became my mantra when I realized I had to work through the life changes that were taking place.

Like Mary, I have become new. Like Barbara, I am filled with gratitude for my life with my husband, for our accomplishments, joys and memories. I am pleased to be where I am today. I am deeply interested in discovering where I will be tomorrow. Like so many in the project, I learned that when my need to look ahead became stronger than my need to look back, I was on my way. With the sharing and help of others, I could make it happen. So can you.

Printed in the United States
46969LVS00001B/5